THE ROAD

A JOURNEY THROUGH THE NARRATIVE OF SCRIPTURE

The Road: A Journey Through the Narrative of Scripture, (3rd Edition)

978-0-6450366-4-0

© The Story Church Project

All rights reserved. No part of this publication may be reproduced, stored in a retrieval system, or transmitted in any form or by any means—for example, electronic, photocopy, recording—without the prior written permission of the author. The only exception is brief quotations.

For permissions or information contact: pastormarcos@thestorychurchproject.com

Cover and Graphic Design by:
Andrew Carroll—www.42Design.co

Edited by Phoenix R. (F_ether) via Fiverr.com

All scripture quotations taken from the World English Bible (WEB) unless otherwise noted.

THE ROAD ONLINE

The following book will take you on a road trip through scripture's overarching plot line. To get the most out of each chapter, download "The Withness App" and watch the accompanying videos.

The Withness App is free to download and the online school is available, also for free, on the app. Once you have logged in, simply tap the menu in the top left, and then scroll down to "The Road Online" for full access.

For those who plan on using these guides for a beginners Bible class at their church, or for one-on-one exploration, go to the same link and watch the video series titled "Navigating."

To begin, scan the QR code below or download the app for Apple or Androind at thewithnessapp.com. Note, this app is for mobile only and is also available in the Apple app store.

SCAN ME

TABLE OF CONTENTS

Introduction 6

PART 1

1. The Beginning 16
2. The Song 24
3. The Fall 32
4. The Book 40
5. The Lamb 48
6. The Cross 58
7. The Gift 66
8. The Restoration 74
9. The Family 86

Pit Stop 94

PART 2

1. The War..................... 104
2. The Empires............ 112
3. The Beast 120
4. The Other................. 130
5. The Reset 138
6. The One 148
7. The Portal 158
8. The Protest............. 168
9. The Remaining 178

Pit Stop............................ 188

PART 3

1. The Signs................. 198
2. The Collapse............ 206
3. The Mark 214
4. The Warnings 224
5. The Return............... 232
6. The Millennium ... 238
7. The Mortals............. 248
8. The Fire 258
9. The Wedding 266

Pit Stop............................276

INTRODUCTION

Imagine moving into a beautiful mansion. It is everything you ever imagined and longed for in a home. Possibilities and exciting anticipations flood your imagination. But then you discover, much to your horror, that the mansion is haunted. What should have been a new chapter of joy has become a nightmare.

This might be the plotline for the 2005 film *The Amityville Horror*, but it is also a fitting description of the human experience. We construct a beautiful life and achieve our dreams, only to nod our heads as John Mayer sings, "somethings missing." So we try hard to get rid of the haunting—to drown it out via distracting amusements and the endless pursuit of more material success. But it keeps coming back like a ghost of longings and moods that can't be ignored. Holocaust survivor and psychiatrist Victor E. Frankl defined this experience as an "existential vacuum," and the great 20th century writer C.S. Lewis understood it as an "other world" craving that nothing in this world could satisfy.

So what do we do with this? One simple approach is to explore the two most common ways in which people attempt to make sense of these longings: the way of *Atheism* and the way of *Theism*. Atheism claims that there is no God and our origin is, therefore, random and unprompted. This basically means that our inner yearning for significance is met by a cold, frigid universe that mocks us with meaninglessness. You might wish for a greater purpose, but the lonely stars assure you no such thing exists. So, in the end, any meaning at all must be self-authored. This simply means you must become the engineer of your own significance. Theism, on the other hand, says we emerge from a conscious being who has a specific purpose to our existence and that the inner longings we experience find their ultimate satisfaction in encountering this creator.

Once a person embraces either belief, the journey is far from over. Atheists have a ton of questions to sort through, such as: How can nothing give birth to something? If I come from nothing, what is my purpose? What about destiny? In the absence of these, where is my value? Can I live as I please? If not, what are the boundaries and who determines them? Why does evil exist? Is there even such a thing?

Theists have their own questions to explore. Once you have embraced the idea of God, you must then ask: Who is this God? And what is it like? Is it an impersonal energy? Or does it have consciousness and personality? If it is evil, does it deserve my attention? And if it is good, why is there evil?

The questions can be exhausting, but the only thing harder is the uphill battle you have to fight to avoid confronting them. Deep within us, there is a haunting desire to make sense of the universe, the world, and the reality of a short conscious existence filled with a longing that nothing seems to satisfy. In short, to avoid taking this journey is more difficult than the journey itself.

That is where this book comes in. If you are reading this, it is most likely because you are exploring the possibility that there is a god and that perhaps this being has communicated with man through the Bible. In this series, we will explore the Bible's narrative that believers regard as the means by which God has spoken to humanity.

However, we don't want this to be some boring, drawn-out religious exercise. So, rather than thinking of this as a "study," think of it as a quest. In the chapters that follow, we will be going on a road trip through the narrative of scripture—the big story that ties the human story together. This big story is broken up into small stories. These small stories are called "doctrines," which simply means "teachings." By exploring the doctrines one by one within the framework of a story, we will cruise through the narrative, pausing long enough to admire the heart of God as it unfolds.

Because this book explores scripture as a journey, it is laid out in "legs," as in a road trip. Each leg (accompanied by one of the above shapes) will introduce you to the story one bit of the road at a time. For example, the first "leg," on God and Creation, will explore the doctrines of who God is, why he created, and what we exist for. The "leg" on War will navigate the doctrines of suffering and sin. Restoration will look at how God rebirths our broken humanity. Empire will explore both the injustice of the church and God's resistance. Protest will survey the alternative community that God is molding against the systemic inequities of our societies and nations. Finally, New Creation will take a brief tour through what God's ultimate restoration of universal oneness will be like. This is the final leg, where our journey ends.

You will need a Bible (or Google) to look up references and a pen to write answers down. At the end of each chapter, you will have the opportunity to explore how the teaching interacts with your life. If you need help with this, or anything else in this book, be sure to watch the online videos at the end of each chapter by scanning the QR code, like the one below.

Also, keep in mind that this adventure doesn't have to be solitary. In fact, it can be more fun when done in community. So as you go on the road trip, ask others to join you or register for our free "Road Live Sessions" via our app below. The companions along this journey are your fellow travelers, and as you explore, you will all grow together, discovering the cosmic panorama of scripture's story—a picture that will change the way you see yourself, the world around you, and everything in between.

GO LIVE!

With that said, it's also a good idea to get yourself a plain journal that you can write in as you go through this series. To begin, write a list of your prime spiritual questions. As you go through this journey, you can flip back to those questions and see how they are being answered. In the end, you will be able to not only make sense of the chaos but also discover the very heart of God—the true fountain that can satisfy our deepest thirst.

More Than Information...

Because the heart of God is our focus, there is one other point that must be understood before we begin. It is impossible for any of us to experience the heart of God by merely reading about it. The only way to truly experience him is to allow the story of scripture to bring us into contact with him, and once there, to wrestle with him, with ourselves, and with the decisions that our encounter is leading us toward. In this sense, the studies you are about to explore cannot be fully appreciated by merely taking information in; rather, it is by expressing our inner, or hidden, self (our intimate thoughts and moods) to God that we can enter into relationship with him. As a result, every chapter concludes with the following acronym to facilitate the experience of unveiling your inner self to God. The acronym is ROAD, and it is a simple prayer-pathway you can do privately as well as with your fellow travelers. It flows like this:

Review — *Take this time to review what the chapter explored. Rephrase and summarize the entire lesson in your own words.*

Open — *Open your heart to God as you would with a friend. Talk about what you discovered and how it is impacting you.*

Ask — *Ask God to make the theme real for you. You don't just want head knowledge, you want experience! You want to feel and truly grasp his heart with your own.*

Decide — *If you are ready, make a decision based on what you discovered. It can be as simple as deciding to think about it more. It can be as deep as reorienting your life and priorities. The point is to be authentic with God and let him handle the rest.*

These prayers are "connect moments," and they are absolutely essential to this voyage. Without them, you can go through the whole journey and walk away with a pretty broad knowledge of the Bible's overarching thematic structure. But it won't make a difference in your life, satisfy your deepest longings, or bring you into a real encounter with your creator. And if you want a true, trans-personal experience that redefines your life, then you cannot skip talking to the very God you are reading about. As you talk to him, you will find that not only are you learning more about him, you are actually getting to know him.

Maybe you have never prayed before, and the whole thing makes you uneasy. The important point to remember is that, in this series, there is no secret formula, special words, or ritualistic pattern to prayer. It really is just opening your heart to God as you do with a friend. Allow the conversation to flow naturally and freely. God isn't interested in perfectly outlined prayers. He is interested in authenticity. In the end, if you are super nervous, ask your fellow travelers to help you. There are also some short videos in the intro to *The Road Online* that talk a bit more about this. You can access them below.

May this book, and the chapters that follow, interact meaningfully with your search for what lies beyond. May you discover that God is not far away but is already with you in this very moment. May you encounter a story so compelling and divine that it rebirths you into a new dimension of existence. May you unveil the heart of your creator and find yourself moving to a new rhythm, guided by a bright north star, and re-created to a new way—his way, not of religion but of relationship with the one whom all your longings point to. Because it is in knowing him that we find everything our hearts are searching for.

ENGAGE

Scan the QR code to watch this section's accompanying Reflection videos.

SCAN ME

A Word on Religious Trauma

Before we close the intro and move into our journey, we need to pause for a moment to consider a theme that will be orbited throughout this book: *religious trauma*. Not everyone reading this book will be a survivor of religious trauma or spiritual abuse, but some might. Because of this, its important to express, from the beginning, that this book recognizes three very important things:

- The church has hurt people. As a result, this book isn't here to defend or make excuses for the church. In part 2 of our journey, we will tackle many of the church's injustices head-on. The goal is for survivors of religious trauma to know they are seen.

- Religious trauma is a real thing. It is not the result of weak faith or a rebellious attitude. It is a real experience caused by abusive church environments.

- Religious trauma is driven by twisted teachings that benefit power over people. In this journey, we are going to benefit people over power—just like Jesus did.

In this book, we are going to explore the narrative of scripture in a trauma-informed, healing-oriented way. This means three simple things:

- We will focus on a new way of seeing God that removes the power dynamics imposed on him by man-made systems and institutions.

- Throughout the book, you will find "Healing Teaching blocks." These blocks are simple pauses that identify a common teaching that causes harm, and then replaces it with the healing truth Jesus came to reveal. (See the first one in the next page!)

- We will explore the Bible's apocalyptic vision with new eyes. Apocalyptic, end-of-the-world trauma is a very real thing. In this book, we will explore these visions in a way that centers the promise of liberation and social justice. This perspective nurtures healing by rejecting fear-driven religion and celebrating God's heart of compassion for all of us.

Despite the above approach, if anything feels triggering as you read, make sure you listen to your body and either pace yourself or put the book down. This book is a spiritual guide, but it is not a replacement for professional therapy or a mental health care plan. So make sure you take the appropriate self-care steps so that you can heal and grow into the beautiful plan God has for you.

HEALING TEACHING

Many people picture God as a coercive tyrant who is distant and angry. These images can have an adverse effect on our mental health because we navigate life with the fear of the angry-god that is out to get us. Spiritual healing begins when we discover that Creator is an eternal community of love who made us to share himself (love) with us, and invites us into an endless relational dance with himself.

As the
deer longs for
streams of water
so I long for you,
O God.

KING DAVID, PSALM 42:1, NLT

PART 1:
1. THE BEGINNING

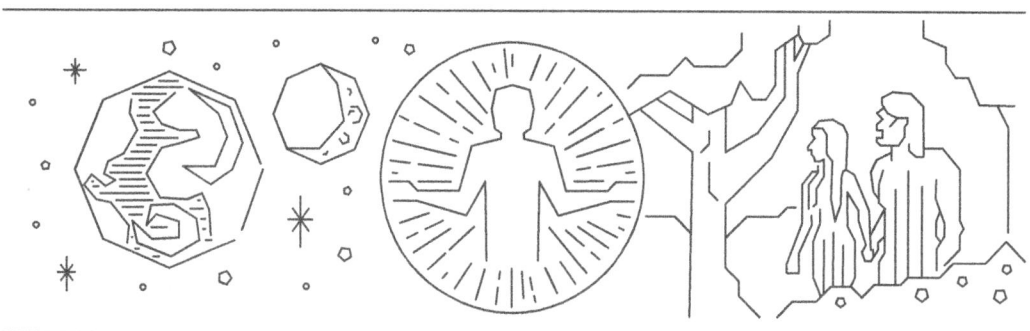

First this: God created the Heavens and Earth—all you see, all you don't see. Earth was a soup of nothingness, a bottomless emptiness, an inky blackness. God's Spirit brooded like a bird above the watery abyss. God spoke: "Light!" And light appeared. (Genesis 1:1–3, The Message)

The story begins. God creating the world and everything in it. This story—recorded in the biblical book of Genesis—is a radical story of origins that differs from many ancient myths and modern cosmologies. In the ancient stories, humanity often comes into being by mistake or to serve as some kind of slave to the gods. In the modern story, our species emerges out of an undirected evolutionary process; any meaning we have we must engineer for ourselves, any value we have is ultimately relative.

However, according to the Bible's creation story, we were brought into being by a divine intelligence—a Great Spirit who transcends all our temporal categories, who has a purpose for each of us that is greater, more adventurous, and more panoramic than our wildest dreams can fathom.

But let's pause for a moment and take a step backward. There are two questions we need to answer before we go any further: The first, who exactly is this creator? The second, why is he creating?

Who is this Creator?

Read 1 John 4:8 and 16. What do these verses tell us about who God is and what he is like? (You can also open up all the chapter's verses by scanning the QR code in the title page)

_____

_____

_____

Chances are your answer has something to do with love. And you would be right, but there is more to God's love than many people realize. The best way to make sense of it is to dig deeper into the original language John used to write those words. Unlike English, the Greek language John used has eight different words for love. Here are three of them:

Φιλέω–philía	Ἔρως–érōs	Ἀγάπη–AGAPE
Friendship between equals, loyalty, family, brotherly love.	Romantic love, especially referring to sexual passion.	Other-centered love especially referring to love with no strings attached.

When John defines Creator as being love, he repeatedly uses "agape". Meaning, this being is, at its very core, an other-centered being. Agape love is all about putting someone else before yourself with no strings attached (1 Corinthians 13:4–7). In other words, God is not an impersonal energy. He is personal. He is relational. And secondly, this God is not selfish. He is always thinking of the "other" and always acts in the best interest of others, not himself.

The story of scripture begins here and nowhere else. *Creator is love.* And before any other thought can be given to the story that is about to unfold, this one foundation needs to be cemented. In the cosmic beginning, we are introduced to a personal divine consciousness who is the very essence of love. And it is through this revelation that the rest of the story unfolds.

However, the love of God presents an immediate contradiction. Agape (other-centered) love is not possible if you exist by yourself. And yet the Bible clearly teaches that God is "one", not "many." One of scripture's faith-fathers—an ancestor named Moses—put it this way:

> "Hear, O Israel: The Lord our God, the Lord is <u>one</u>."
> *(Deuteronomy 6:4, NIV)*

And here is the contradiction: If God existed before anything else existed that means that there was a time when he was all alone—nothing to love or to love him in return. So then, is it possible for Creator to be the very essence of selfless love if he existed all by himself before anything was created? Notice, the Bible doesn't say God started loving once he created. It says he was love from eternity past. This means that he has always been other-centered love. But how was he "other-centered" if he existed when there was no "other"?

Read Genesis 1:26. In this verse God refers to himself as "us". What does this mean? Read also John 1:1–3, 14–17; Matthew 28:19; and John 14:16–17, 23. What are these verses suggesting?

In the Bible, God is presented as being both three and one at the same time. The Father is God, Jesus is God, and the Holy Spirit is God. All three of them are separate and yet one. Because of this, Jesus could say, "I and the Father are one." (John 10:30)

But how do we make sense of this? How can God be both three and one at the same time? Notice, the Bible doesn't teach there are three Creators. There is only one. It also does not teach that the one God manifests in three different ways. The Father, Son, and Holy Spirit are not three separate versions of the same God. They are each uniquely themselves, and yet they are one. But isn't this illogical? How can one be three, and three be one?

This concept is admittedly one of the most mysterious teachings in the Bible, and for good reason. We cannot put God in a test tube or in a box that we are comfortable with. He is greater and more transcendent than we could ever imagine. But as mysterious as this teaching may be, we must keep in mind that the rules of our physical universe do not apply to God. He exists outside of our dimension and its inherent limits. So, what is impossible for us due to the limitations of physics is possible for him. He is three and one.

But we don't have to look too far from our own observable universe to get a clearer picture of how God can be this mysterious collective consciousness of three beings who are also one. Our own world has really strange things taking place in its "basement" that scientists can observe but struggle to explain. Take the following quantum phenomenons as an example:

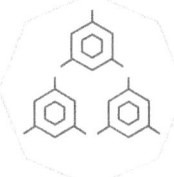

ENTANGLEMENT
When particles stay connected to each other despite being apart.

SUPERPOSITION
When a particle appears in more than one place at the same time.

NON-CAUSALITY
When events take place simultaneously instead of before and after.

Now, if you're not a science nerd the above examples might be confusing, so think of it like this: Imagine a chair in your dining room that moves whenever I move a chair in my dining room. Despite no apparent physical connection, somehow when I move my chair, yours moves too. That's entanglement. Or, imagine a cat in your house that also happens to live in my house and your grandma's house at the same time, despite us living miles away from each other. That's superposition. Or, imagine walking into my house only to find you were already there, and when you turn around to leave you discover you are only just arriving. That's non-causality.

Does your brain hurt yet? Hopefully. Even Albert Einstein was weirded out by these observations. In fact, he is known to have referred to quantum physics as the "spooky" science. But as bizarre as these scenarios might be, scientists observe them in the quantum realm very regularly. So if things that make no sense in our physical dimension can still take place in our own observable universe, its possible for a god who transcends all these dimensions to be infinitely more mysterious—including the mind-boggling, radical idea that he is both three and one at the same time.

But why does this matter? Because, if its true, then Creator is community and always has been. This shows that he is indeed the essence of selfless love. He has existed as a triune being for all eternity in an eternal relationship of agape love. He has always been in relationship; he has always given and received love. Before anything else was created, the Father, Son, and Spirit lived in a symbiotic relationship of reciprocal love. The Father gave to the Son, the Son to the Spirit, and vice versa. God is a social unit who has lived in eternal other-centeredness—giving and receiving love.

Why Did He Create Us?

But the question remains, why did God create us?

Was he bored? Lonely? Did he need slaves to do his dirty work? Or was he perhaps looking to create beings who could feed his fragile ego with songs about his greatness? Is God the most needy being in the universe?

Read Isaiah 43:7. This text seems to imply that God is indeed an egocentric being who wants to be worshiped. Compare it with Acts 17:24–25 and share your thoughts:

God doesn't need anything. That's what Acts tells us. He wasn't needy. He wasn't bored. He wasn't lonely. He didn't need slaves. And he didn't need people to tell him how cool he is. God is not unstable or needy. So then why did he create us?

Only one logical conclusion remains. If God did not create us to *get* something from us, he must have created us to *give* something to us. The "glory" Isaiah speaks of is a reference to the *love* of God. God's glory lies in who he is, and love is the definition of who he is. He did not create us to receive something from us that he didn't already have. He created us to give something to us—he made us for his love. And it is this revelation that gives us the clearest answer to our existence. We exist to be the recipients of God's eternal love.

Shabbat and Meaning...

The greatest evidence of this is found in the creation story itself. According to Genesis, when God completed his work of creation he "he rested… from all his work of creation which he had done" (Genesis 2:2). Now of course, God doesn't get tired. The humans weren't tired either, they had only been alive for one day. So, this act of rest is not about recovering from exhaustion. It's about something more.

The Hebrew word for rest is "shabbat" and when God rested on the seventh day he was declaring his relational desire to be close to humanity. To enjoy us and the ecosystem of beauty and purpose he had designed. In this story, man does not exist to be a divine slave or puppet. Rather, we exist within a purposefully designed interconnectedness, a oneness that flows via reciprocal and relational love. This means, we do not have to manufacture meaning or purpose for ourselves. Our meaning is deeply rooted in the heart of God, who made us to be in relationship with him and to experience the boundless adventure of his eternal community of love.

REFLECT

Creator is love. He is three in one—an eternal, self-existent community. He did not create because he was needy. He created out of the overflow of his communal love. Mankind was made in his image—the image of love—for the express purpose of living forever in selfless love with one another and with him. The image of God, our creator, forever answers the questions of purpose, destiny, and value that have plagued humanity for millennia. This perfect relational being created us for a relational purpose. His first gift to humanity was to "shabbat," or "rest," with his creation as an act of intimacy. In all of this we discover why we exist: *to love and be loved.*

CONNECT

Review _____

_____

Open _____

_____

Ask _____

_____

Decide _____

_____

ENGAGE

Scan the QR code to watch this chapter's accompanying Reflection video.

SCAN ME: THE BEGINNING

2. THE SONG

God is love. From this simple starting point, the rest of scripture's narrative begins to unfold with beauty and intrigue. Creator, it turns out, is community, and he is love. He speaks the universe into existence, crafts galaxies, and breathes stars. Then, according to Genesis, he speaks again and the only world you and I have ever known is born.

"Good"

Over and over in Genesis 1, the author, Moses, uses the Hebrew word "tov," which means "good," to communicate the perfection of God's artwork. Seven times we read, "and God saw that it was good." Then, as creation ends with Adam and Eve, the text tells us, "God saw that it was very good." *Tov* and very *tov*. That was the world God made for us. It was good and very good in every imaginable way. And while we don't know everything about this original ecosystem, Genesis introduces us to three basic themes that help us step into our purpose as human beings. Understanding this is important because, while the nature of God's love informs *why* we exist, the rhythms present in his creation tell us *what* we were created to do.

So, what are the three basic themes? Let's explore one at a time.

Read Genesis 1:26–28 and Genesis 2:4–8, 15. What pattern of life do these verses introduce us to?

_____
_____
_____

According to the story, Adam and Eve were created to "rule" the earth and to "subdue" it. In other words, they had a purpose. While the world was perfect, they were not created to wander around with nothing to do. They had an assignment. The earth was a symbiotic network, and they were its caretakers.

But Genesis 2 reveals something unexpected. Part of our planet, it seems, is not fully cultivated. Eden's natural cycle appears complete, but beyond we are given a picture of a world in need of a gardener. This was Adam and Eve's role. Not only did they nurture the animal kingdom, their purpose was to co-cultivate with God. And from this purpose, we are introduced to the second theme.

Read Genesis 1:28 and Genesis 2:18–25. What else do these verses reveal about God's original intent in creation?

_____
_____
_____

"Not Good"

For the first time in the creation story, we are introduced to something that is not good. Adam is not meant to be alone. Together, the Bible says man and woman form the image of God, (Genesis 1:27), and together they are to mine beauty from the earth. Theirs is the first human relationship. But notice that this relationship finds its meaning in something that transcends its own immediacy. Adam and Eve, together, are to take an uncultivated world and turn it into something beautiful. Through co-creation, synergy, and oneness of purpose, the first human relationship models both our individual and collective purpose as a species. We exist to make the world more beautiful. You and I are multipliers of beauty, world makers at our very core. As a result, no matter how much success and pleasure we accumulate to ourselves, we will never find meaning in life until we inhabit this original purpose for which we exist.

To put it simply, a life that does not beautify the earth is a meaningless life, irrespective of how much material and experiential trinkets it acquires. At our very center, we humans are social, spiritual, and planetary gardeners.

A God who Celebrates...

So far, we have seen two themes in the story of Genesis. First, mankind was created to fulfill a purpose. We were not created to wander aimlessly in lazy bliss. This foundation shows us that the dreams and desires of our hearts are part of God's original design. He created us to think big, and whenever we settle for anything other than his will for us, a part of us is lost. But we have also seen that God designed us to fulfill our purpose in relationship. Through community and connection, mankind is to make a beautiful world. This foundation calls us to orient our lives with wisdom, always thinking about how we can cultivate the beauty of our world and neighborhoods, not just our own desires.

But there is one more theme to explore. Unlike what many ancient myths suggest, the God of Genesis did not create man to till the earth as his slaves. Their gardening was to give them purpose in life, not use them to accomplish something God didn't want to do himself. And nowhere in Genesis is this truth reinforced more than in Genesis 2:1–3.

Read Genesis 2:1–3, Exodus 20:8–11, and Mark 2:27. What do these verses tell us about God's relationship with man?

As we saw in the previous chapter, *shabbat* is introduced in Genesis 2, where God "rested" from all his work. Exodus then helps us understand the original purpose for this day of rest. Through this weekly moment in time, God aims to remind us that we, and all of creation, are valuable and designed for relationship, not for the endless rounds of production and consumption. Jesus seals the deal when he tells us that the "Sabbath was made for man" (Mark 2:27)—a gift from our creator to remind us that, while we have a purpose in life, our work is never to replace our relationships with each other, and most importantly with him.

Purpose | Connection | Celebration

So far, we have seen three overarching themes in the original creation: Our "Purpose" (to make the earth more beautiful), our "Connection" (to birth beauty through community), and God's "Celebration" (Shabbat as a reminder that we are loved for who we are, not what we produce).

Each of these themes is vitally important, not only to the audience Moses is writing to—an audience surrounded by unjust hierarchies, social inequity, and economic exploitation—but also to us. Our age is currently steeped in fragmented narratives leaving many of us confused about our significance as human beings. Today, it seems many presume our existence has no true or lasting magnitude. The beauty of our natural world is repeatedly exploited, relationships viewed as means to personal gain, and in this milieu, we, who were made in the image of God, emerge as mere commodities for corporate gain—the opposite of shabbat.

But agape love is the way God designed creation, and everything in it, to operate. So, think of God's creation as a beautiful orchestra. So long as humanity was in connection to him, the song was beautiful. Each note in its rightful place. The rhythm and harmony flowed perfectly. Man, woman, and God in intimate, rhythmic connection with one another and the world around them. There was no discord in the song. No interruption. No note was out of tune, no tempo out of sync.

This was God's original design, and the laws that governed his creation were engineered to compose this song of agape love, that echoed in every society and culture. Had it remained untainted, human civilization would have flourished into a multi-cultural, multi-planetary community governed by a rhythm in synchronicity with God's own heart.

Think about the three existential themes of Genesis 1–2 (Purpose, Connection, Celebration) and how together they compose a song of meaning and beauty. Then, with that song in mind, read Jeremiah 29:11. What does this text mean for your life right now?

_____
_____
_____

HEALING TEACHING

Human social structures are often hierarchical, placing some people at the top of a power-pyramid and others at the bottom. Ideas like patriarchy, racial superiority, misogyny, and misandry are among the most common we see today, even in faith communities. But the story of creation shows that God's original design was one of co-creation, a circle of relational oneness and harmony in all creation. Rather than a cosmic emperor at the top who takes from those below him (us) God is like the roots of a tree that serve and nurture the branches, producing good fruit.

REFLECT

God created a perfect world. But this perfect world was not a fairytale kind of dream. Rather, it was a very real world with real people doing real work. Adam and Eve, the first relationship, had a mutual purpose to make a beautiful world as co-cultivators. As they engaged in this purpose, they fulfilled their individual and collective meaning as human beings. This pattern of purpose was to repeat each week, leading to shabbat—a day which God set aside as a special day of rest to celebrate humanity's value and relationship with all things. All of this points to God's heart of love, but it also points to God's original design of a song that, to this day, can bring harmony and synchronicity to our fragmented lives.

CONNECT

Review _____

_____

Open _____

_____

Ask _____

_____

Decide _____

_____

ENGAGE

Scan the QR code to watch this chapter's accompanying Reflection video.

SCAN ME: THE SONG

3. THE FALL

In the beginning God created the world. (Genesis 1–2) It was perfect. Perfect love. Perfect harmony. Perfect relationships. There was no death, suffering, or pain. Mankind was happy and at peace. Today life is no longer like this. Love has been replaced by selfishness. Equality by discrimination. Injustice and oppression strangle our societies. Addiction tears families apart. Relationships fail and death separates us from those we love. In short, we live in a fractured, broken world. But if God didn't create it this way, what happened?

The answer is found in the story we are exploring. So far, we have seen that the story begins with who God is and what he created us for. The story continues in Genesis 3:

> *The serpent was the shrewdest of all the wild animals the Lord God had made. One day he asked the woman, "Did God really say you must not eat the fruit from any of the trees in the garden? "Of course we may eat fruit from the trees in the garden," the woman replied. "It's only the fruit from the tree in the middle of the garden that we are not allowed to eat. God said, 'You must not eat it or even touch it; if you do, you will die.'" (Genesis 3:1–3, NLT)*

Pause.

Something strange is happening here. This verse raises more questions than it answers. First, why was there a talking serpent? Second, why was there a forbidden tree? And third, how does this help make sense of the brokenness in our world?

Why Was there a Talking Serpent?

Let's answer these three questions in order. To do so, we need to go back to the first chapter of the story—the one in which we encountered the character and essence of God as other-centered, agape, love. This love is the central truth that helps us make sense of everything else in the Bible. God is love and he created out of the overflow of his love. This is why John the Apostle could say, "He who doesn't love doesn't know God, for God is love" (1 John 4:8).

God's love is not mere sentimental emotion. It is deeper than that. It is other-centeredness. It always acts on behalf of the other, never on behalf of itself. However, in order for God to create a reality that operated according to this kind of love there had to be freedom. Without freedom, love cannot exist. But of course, with freedom comes the risk that someone will choose not to love in return.

An illustration might be of help here. Suppose you fall in love. Whenever you see that other person, butterflies erupt in your stomach. You just have to get to know them. So, one day, you approach this special someone and, without asking, immediately place a micro-chip behind their ear that programs their brain to "love" you. At that moment, your crush turns around, looks deeply into your eyes, and declares their love for you. After dating for some time, there is a proposal, and lifelong marriage follows.

Would you call this a love story worthy of its own "romance" novel?

Perhaps it would make a good book, but "psychological thriller" might be a more fitting genre. Authentic love is "other-focused." It places the other person above self. As a result, true love cannot be programmed, reduced to an algorithm, or scripted. The moment it is, the person ceases to be a person. They become a cybernetic device acting on automated commands. Love, in order to be real, must flow within an autonomous, organic exchange. And it is this liberty that leaves the door wide open for someone to freely choose not to love in return.

Read Ezekiel 28:12–17; Isaiah 14:12–15; Luke 10:18; and Revelation 12:9. Who and what are these verses talking about?

_____

_____

_____

These passages introduce us to scripture's main antagonist—a character most often referred to as "the Satan" (a Hebrew noun meaning "the accuser"). According to the story, this once-perfect angel (commonly known as "Lucifer") chose to rebel against God. God did not create evil. It was Lucifer's choice as a free, moral agent. The Bible reveals that, as a result of that choice, a war broke out in heaven and eventually spread to earth. And it was through the medium of the serpent that the Satan made his next move.

Why Was there a Forbidden Tree?

Suppose a friend took you shopping and promised to buy you whatever you wanted, would you take them up on the offer? Chances are, yes. But then, what would you say if, after choosing all your favorite items, your friend said, "No, I am not going to buy this," and proceeded to replace everything you chose with "better" choices. Would you protest? Would you say, "Didn't you say I could choose whatever I wanted?"

But, what if your friend said to you, "I did say you could choose whatever you wanted, but my choices for you are so much better." What would you say then? In case you have no answer, consider this one: *If you are not free to have what you choose, are you really free to choose it in the first place? Or is your choice merely an illusion?*[1]

Because love demands freedom, we also have a choice. God did not silence the Satan, nor does he manipulate us. The tree in the garden allowed this cosmic rebel to have a voice, and this in itself is a reflection of God's government of love. Although he warned Adam and Eve of the consequences of consuming the fruit of the tree, he did not remove their choice to do so.

Read Genesis 3:4–7. What happens next?

_____
_____
_____

Notice, God did not slap the fruit from Eve's hand. Eve was free to eat the fruit. Her choice was not an illusion. God meant what he said. His government is a government of love, and love demands freedom in order to be authentic.

How Does this Help Make Sense of the Brokenness in Our World?

There is more happening in this story than just a talking serpent and a forbidden tree. When humanity chose to distrust God they opted to disconnect themselves from the source of life. And in doing so, a natural consequence would follow. God had warned, "You may freely eat of every tree of the garden; but you shall not eat of the tree of the knowledge of good and evil; for in the day that you eat of it, you will surely die" (Genesis 2:16–17).

Now, of course no one dropped dead the moment the fruit was eaten. We will discuss why in more detail as the story progresses.

But for now, one thing is clear—from that moment something in the nature of reality changed. Adam and Eve experienced fear and shame. They had unplugged themselves from the only true source of all that is good and just. Immediately following their sin, Adam and Eve could no longer be in the presence of God. They were removed from the garden and entered a new experience of separation. And like an apple, plucked from its branch and left in the sun, life withers and decays until all that is left are the moldy ashes of what could have been. The ultimate end of this decay is death, but in between we experience all its side effects: wars, famines, suffering, disease, heartbreak, injustice, disaster, oppression, and violence.

But why would God allow this? Why create Lucifer in the first place? And from there, why not destroy him the moment he rebelled? And the same questions can be asked of humanity as well.

The answer is really simple when we look through the lens of other-centered love. Remember, love in the Bible is not a sentimental concept. It is a foundational principle. It is self-sacrifice, self-abandonment, and self-giving. This is the very opposite of our fallen nature, which is self-centered, self-focused, and self-promoting. God's government is designed in harmony with his own nature of other-focused love. And as a result, everything God does he does as an expression of this love. God does not sit in heaven and decide who gets to exist based on who will love him and who won't. To do so would be manipulative. God did not destroy the Satan right away because he is not a dictator. He desires authentic and autonomous relationships. And he cannot have a universe that operates this way if everyone is afraid to question him. The same answers apply to the rebellion that happened on this planet.

However, just because God did not destroy this emerging antagonist right away does not mean that God is silent. The Bible declares that God knows the end from the beginning (Isaiah 46:10), that all of reality is held together by him (Colossians 1:16–17) and that he knows no equal. (Psalm 97:9) As a result, God was not caught by surprise and he is no victim. God has the upper hand and he has never abandoned us. The rest of the story of scripture is a journey into how God reverses the separation and discord that sin caused and restores the universe back to oneness and harmony.

---

1. Illustration credit: Herb Montgomery, founder of *Renewed Heart Ministries*.

HEALING TEACHING

The biblical doctrine of "sin" is one of the most misused teachings in scripture. Weaponised by harmful religious institutions, cults, and toxic faith communities this teaching is used to shame and control. Biblically, however, the concept of sin is intended to disempower shame and liberate us from religion's behavioural shackles. If we are fallen, we can be kind to ourselves in the midst of our imperfections, failures, and shortfalls. If we are deeply loved in our fallenness, we can look beyond the wounded-self to see what God sees—a beautiful sacred being whose company he longs for. The teaching of sin is a liberating realization that calls us to be kind to ourselves and to recognize that God's love for us—not shame—is the very thing that can heal and restore us.

REFLECT

God did not create sin. Because God is love, he created us with the freedom of choice. We can choose either life with God or life apart from God. By joining the Satan in his rebellion, our first parents chose life apart from God. In doing so they introduced sin into God's perfect creation. Sin separated man from God and is the cause of all the suffering in this world. Ultimately, it leads to death. But it doesn't end there. Creator, the story says, now activates an ancient and mysterious plan to restore the universe back to the harmony and oneness for which it was designed.

CONNECT

Review _____
_____

Open _____
_____

Ask _____
_____

Decide _____
_____

ENGAGE

Scan the QR code to watch this chapter's accompanying Reflection video.

SCAN ME: THE FALL

4. THE BOOK

The fall changed everything. Once sin enters the human experience, the story tells us they were filled with fear and shame and "hid themselves from the presence of God" (Genesis 3:8). The nature of reality changed. The other-centered design of the cosmos was interrupted by a toxic vibration that violated the harmony of the ecosystem. So God had to do something that was never supposed to happen. Adam and Eve were sent "*out* from the garden of Eden..." (Genesis 3:22), the rhythms of "with" disrupted by the introduction of "out."

This banishment from the garden must have been painful for God. But that was not the worst part. The worst part was that while God's presence would have filled Adam and Eve with joy before the fall, it now filled them with fear. After the fall, we are told that those who saw even a glimpse of God trembled and fainted. God even went so far as to say: "man may not see me and live" (Exodus 33:20).

Sin separated humanity from Creator and threatens to keep us separated forever. This separation is so intense that—like opposing magnetic forces—we cannot enter his presence. If we tried, the Bible says we would be overwhelmed. Therefore, there was no way for us to approach God with a solution to the problem. However, the Bible reveals something else about God that is just as foundational as his love and that will help to unravel the rest of the story.

Look up Exodus 25:8; 2 Samuel 22:7; and Psalm 48:9. What are these texts talking about?

_____
_____
_____

Next to the love of God, the sanctuary is one of the biggest themes in the Bible. It resides in heaven (Hebrews 9:24), and a copy of it was made on earth (Exodus 25:8–9), serving as Israel's center of worship. However, in order to really grasp the significance of the sanctuary its important, at this point, to think of it not as a building made of stones and jewels, but as a theme or posture in God's heart. And while the sanctuary is a multivariate phenomenon, it can be boiled down to one simple concept: *God's desire to be with us.*

What this means is that the sanctuary isn't ultimately about a building, but about God's eternal desire to be close to us. It is not enough for God to be creator. He also wants to be friend. What this means is that God not only loves you; he likes you. He created you, yes. But more specifically, he wants to be close to you. This is what the sanctuary theme of scripture represents: relational oneness and intimacy between creature and creator.

So, with the separation caused by sin, God had to do something. Somehow, he had to reach out to us and reveal to us how much he desires to be with us. But how could God do this? How could he reach out to us with enough power to reveal himself to us, while at the same time holding back enough so as to not overwhelm us?

Read the following verses and write down the different ways in which God has reached out to humanity: Psalm 19:1–4; Numbers 12:6; Daniel 10:11–12; Hebrews 1:2; 2; Peter 3:2.

_____
_____
_____

God has spoken to us through nature, prophets, angels, Jesus, and the apostles. However, there is a weakness in each of these. Nature can only reveal so much. Prophets and apostles do not live forever. Angels are generally only seen in extreme circumstances. And Jesus returned to heaven after his ascension. So, while God communicated through each of these, he still needed a way of revealing his heart to the whole world that would be permanent and accessible. This is why Jesus, as he prepared for his departure, said, "the Counselor, the Holy Spirit, whom the Father will send in my name, will teach you all things, and will remind you of all that I said to you" (John 14:26).

The Holy Spirit dwells with us as a representative of Jesus, who the angel said would be called "Immanuel," which means "God with us", (Matthew 1:23). This sanctuary-God, who loves to be close to us, has never abandoned us despite our rebellion. And through the Holy Spirit, he has provided the best means to communicate his love for us.

Read 2 Timothy 3:15–17; Romans 15:4; and 2 Peter 1:20–21. What are these verses speaking of?

_____
_____
_____

The scriptures (commonly known as the "Bible") are the primary means by which God has chosen to communicate his love to the whole world. They are safe, permanent, accessible, and reveal his heart to all times and cultures. In the Bible, we find the ultimate revelation of who God is, what he is like, and his will for all of us. This is why David, the poet, could say, "your word is a lamp to my feet" (Psalm 119:105).

The word Bible is an ancient word (*biblia*) that simply means "books." This is fitting because the Bible is not one book. It is actually a compilation of 66 books written by about 40 different authors over the course of nearly 1500 years.

The Bible is divided into two sections: The Old Testament (OT) and the New Testament (NT). The OT is primarily the story of Israel—a nation God especially chose to communicate his story to humanity. The New Testament is primarily the story of Jesus and the church, which serve the same purpose as Israel in the OT. However, while there are two sections to the Bible, there is still only one story. The OT and the NT are both parts of the same narrative. In fact, large portions of the NT are quotations from the OT and the plot of the NT is really the continuation of the OT storyline. In a sense, the OT is part one of the story while the NT is part two.

OLD TESTAMENT   NEW TESTAMENT

Story of Israel   *Story of the Church*

Read and discuss 2 Peter 1:20–21 and Psalm 119:105. What do these verses say about God's self-revelation?

_____
_____
_____

How do we know this book can be trusted? Read and ponder 2 Timothy 3:16; 2 Peter 1:19; and Proverbs 30:5.

_____
_____
_____

While the Bible is a human book written by everyday people, its story is ultimately Creator's story and is a portal to his heart. However, trusting the Bible is not something that can be achieved by reading a few verses about trusting the Bible. Trust is something that must be earned with time. But the beauty of scripture is that it introduces us to a sanctuary-God. He is not an impersonal energy or a distant and cold emperor. He wants to be with us, so he promised, "You will seek Me and find Me when you search for Me with all your heart" (Jeremiah 29:13, NIV).

Why a Book?

But why a book? Why doesn't God simply show up and introduce himself? Some skeptics go so far as to say, "If God wants me to believe in him, why not show up in the clouds and say 'Hi, I am God'?" But as we have already seen, in an unstable system like ours (due to the impact of sin) the presence of God is too overwhelming, and potentially dangerous. If God were to appear the way the skeptic asks, you might not survive the event. However, through the stories of the Bible, God has given us the best means by which we can come to know his heart.

To understand this a bit more, look through the following verses and follow the journey they take you on: Exodus 33:20; Judges 13:22; Isaiah 6:5; John 3:12 and 16:12; and 1 Corinthians 13:12.

_____

_____

Now that you have read each of those verses, the following illustration should help it all come together. Suppose you are sitting in a dark room for a whole week. There is not a single ray of light. It is pitch black. When the week ends you feel your way to the door and open it. As soon as you open it, the sun in all its brightness shines directly onto you. What would you do? If you are a normal human being, you would probably be in agony and fall back into the darkness. To go from darkness to light so suddenly would be too much, too soon. Rather than enjoy the beauty of the light you have lived without, you would crawl back into the darkness for fear of going blind.

But what if, when you opened the door, a long hallway with a dim light bulb stretched out before you? Chances are, your eyes would soon adjust to the new light. Then you would walk to the end of the hall and open a new door where another hall with a brighter light would greet you. The process repeats itself so that when you open the final door and the sunshine hits your face, your eyes are fully adjusted, and you can appreciate the bright panoramic canvass before you.

The difference between the two scenarios is simple. In the first, you encountered too much light too soon. In the second, you progressively encountered more and more light until you were finally ready to enjoy the full display of the sun. And this is exactly how the Bible works. While we cannot now enter directly into the presence of God without being overwhelmed, the Bible reveals his glory in stories, poems, and dreams; with the goal of adjusting our spiritual eyes, so that when we finally see him, we will be prepared to enjoy the full display.

In other words, the whole point of scripture's story is that God is working to reverse the damage caused by the fall. "With" was replaced by "out" when humanity was displaced from the garden. But God doesn't want us *out*, he wants us *with*. And through scripture, he aims to bring us back into his sanctuary so that we can be "with" again.

REFLECT

The Bible is a story from God. While written by human beings, it was inspired by God, so that what is written emerges as God's self-revelation. This means the book is both a biography and an autobiography of God. It contains both the experiences and emotions of the human authors and the divine. Through their small stories, these men and women in the Bible point us to a big story—the story of God. Through this story, God leads us, little by little, toward himself, with the aim of reversing the separation between us and restoring us to oneness with his heart.

CONNECT

Review _____
_____

Open _____
_____

Ask _____
_____

Decide _____
_____

ENGAGE

Scan the QR code to watch this chapter's accompanying Reflection video.

SCAN ME: THE BOOK

5. THE LAMB

In the last few chapters, we explored the heart of God as the origin of life and reality. His creation, the laws and patterns that govern it, and his motives behind our existence all flow from his other-centered love. We also saw that God is community (Trinity), and in making us in his image, he designed us for communion with himself, each other, and the earth. But then we are introduced to sin—and everything changes.

The concept of sin doesn't trend in the modern age. For some, the term carries a lot of pathological baggage. It has been used to dehumanize, degrade, and control. It also carries a cynical air with it—almost as if to embrace it would lead someone to adopt a dark, twisted view of themselves. All this is partly true. Sin has been misused, co-opted by religious elites who aim to build their empires by monetizing on humanities guilt and shame. But if we lay all that aside and aim to capture a clearer vision of what the Bible calls sin, things begin to make a little more sense.

A Violation of Design

In its most basic essence, sin is a violation of design. God designed reality to move to the rhythm of love. But when sentient beings (like Adam and Eve) detached themselves from God, they introduced a mysterious tear in the fabric of reality. This tear in the cosmos has destabilized the human being and, really, all of creation. The system is still there, God is still present, goodness is still within us, but the network of reality is now broken. The effects of this tear echo through time, are passed on from generation to generation, and manifest a new way of being in the world. This new way is the way you and I are born into. It is the way of power, injustice, and separation. By rejecting God, man placed himself at the center of himself. Community with God and each other is broken. Selfishness and violence fill a world created for other-centered relationships. And the worst part is that there is nothing we can do to fix it.

Read Romans 3:23. What does it say about the human condition?

_____
_____
_____

Romans says we are sinners. This places us in a scary place for the "wages of sin is death" (Romans 6:23). The separation sin causes not only breaks our community with God and each other during our life—it breaks community for eternity. But remember that the story of scripture isn't actually about us, it's about God. From this perspective, it becomes clear that sin doesn't simply affect us, it affects him. He birthed us for community, and now that community is broken. There could be no worse thing for a God who created us to "sanctuary" with him.

Centuries after the fall, Isaiah, the prophet, described the effects of the sin virus this way: "For we have all become like one who is unclean, and all our righteousness is like a polluted garment. We all fade like a leaf; and our iniquities, like the wind, take us away" (Isaiah 64:6). The Hebrew word translated to "polluted garment" is "tame," which is also used to refer to the carcass of a dead animal. This doesn't mean that we humans are somehow without virtue or beautiful potential. What it does mean is that, when it comes to repairing the tear within us and the reality we inhabit, the very best we have to offer isn't all that great. As positive and enthusiastic as our dreams, successes, and legacies might be, nothing we do comes remotely close to ending the separation and healing our fragmented world.

Read and discuss Psalm 14:3, 51:5, 58:3; Ecclesiastes 7:20; and Romans 3:10–11. How do you relate to what these verses are saying?

_____
_____
_____

From there, turn to Mark 7:21–23 and James 1:14.
Finally, turn to Matthew 22:37–40; Romans 13:10; and 1 John 3:4.
How do these verses help us understand exactly what sin is?

_____
_____
_____

Don't miss this vital point. Sin is not simply doing bad things. Sin is much deeper than that. Sin is lovelessness. Because love is other-centered, sin is, by definition, self-centeredness. Our hearts are stuck in an egocentric loop from birth. This lust for the supremacy of the self is what leads us to manifest toxic cycles in our homes and communities, which are at odds with the law of love. In short, we are not sinners simply because we sin. We sin because we are sinners—born out of harmony with design. Thus, sin is not simply an issue of behavior; it is an issue of the heart. If there is to be any solution to this impasse, it must address our fallen heart, not just our negative behavioral cycles.

Read Isaiah 1:1–6; Romans 7:14–24; Jeremiah 2:22, 13:23, 17:9; and Romans 3:20. Is it possible for us to heal this condition?

_____

_____

_____

This spiritual void consumes us so deeply that self-rescue is impossible. It would be like trying to climb out of a deep chasm that doesn't have a floor or walls. And, like opposing magnetic forces, God's perfect, other-centered love and our self-centered, existential vacuum cannot coexist. Thus, humanity is destined to eternal separation from God; resulting in a permanently, unstable society governed by an impulse of self-preservation that will forever bar us from achieving the harmonious global village we instinctively long for. But it gets worse: Because sin is an issue of the heart, no amount of good behavior can make up for its presence in our lives. Church, religion, education, discipline, moral strictness, self-denial, social action, self-actualization, legislation, rehabilitation, and humanitarian service—even the law of God—are all good things, but they are unable to restore us from sin's brokenness to God's original design.

Enter the Lamb...

Let's pause here for a moment and remember the narrative. God of love. An eternal community of three co-eternal beings who are one. Creation flows from this eternal community, the eternal "one". Sin enters the narrative as the breaking of the oneness—the community reality is designed for. It damages the human heart and we are powerless to do anything about it. Even our best actions are tainted by its miasma. We cannot be in relationship with God. We cannot even live in harmony with his design-law. Our condition is terminal. It is the breeding ground of injustice—the epicenter of pain, suffering and despair.

It is clear that the solution cannot come from humanity. So, if there is to be any solution, it must, of necessity, come from beyond human capacity—it must come from God.

Read Genesis 3 and zoom in on verses 15 and 21. What do these texts say?

_____

_____

Notice verse 15. In it God foretells that one of the woman's descendants would "crush" the serpent's head. In other words, the serpent would be defeated. God then clothes Adam and Eve with "skin" as a metaphor of something that would take place on their behalf. But what exactly is this metaphor all about?

Moses answers this question in chapters 1–7 of the book of Leviticus. The images and description below summarize what Moses says:

LAMB   SANCTUARY   SACRIFICE

The book of Leviticus is the most in-depth exploration of the "sanctuary" found in scripture. In this "sanctuary," God reveals his plan to once again live among us. Because the central theme of the sanctuary is God's desire to be close to us, it makes sense that in it God would reveal how he would accomplish this goal, despite the separation caused by sin.

Now, the book of Leviticus is complex. It deals with sin's existential and spiritual phenomenon in multicolor. It also does so in metaphors and archetypes that would have made sense to the cultural context that the ancient Hebrews inhabited, which makes the book as a whole a bit enigmatic for us in the modern era. However, there is a simple way of summarizing Leviticus. The book is an instruction manual on how an out-of-design (separated) community could re-enter into relational oneness with God.

Think of this process as a play. When a person sinned, they were to take a spotless lamb to the sanctuary. Once inside, they would go to the altar, place their hands on the lamb's head, and transfer the guilt of their sin onto the lamb. The priest would then place the lamb on the altar and the sinner would kill it. Once the blood was shed, the sinner could go home forgiven. In other words, a spotless and innocent lamb would absorb the sinners separation, and then enter into a state of permanent separation (death) on the sinners behalf.

The first time this ever happened was in Genesis 3:21. God dressed Adam and Eve in "skin," meaning something had died, and their "nakedness" (or guilt) was covered by the "skin" of the animal that had been slain in their place. The eternal separation that should have befallen humanity in the aftermath of detaching themselves from God instead fell on an innocent creature, whose life is traded for man's. In short, mankind has never fully experienced the complete effects of separation because something has taken our place. In Genesis, it was an unspecified animal. In Leviticus, it was a lamb. But how can the death of an innocent animal possibly fix the sin problem of divine-human separation?

Read Hebrews 10:4 for the answer. Once you have discussed it, look up John 1:29. What story do these verses tell?

_____

_____

_____

John referred to Jesus as "the Lamb." In other words, all of the animals in the OT were merely metaphors and shadows pointing to a greater reality. That greater reality is Jesus. Jesus is the true lamb who takes away the sin of the world. Though innocent of sin, he absorbed our separation and reversed it. In doing so, Jesus became the bridge to restored oneness with God. But how exactly is Jesus the solution to the spiritual vacuum of sin?

Read and ponder the following verses: John 3:16; 1 Peter 1:18–20; 1 John 2:2; Luke 19:10; 1 Timothy 1:15; and Isaiah 43:25. What do they reveal about God's solution to our separation from him?

_____

_____

_____

The incredible mystery of scripture is that Jesus is not merely a sacrifice that God sent to the earth for sin. To the contrary, Jesus is God. The reason why this is so mysterious is because the Triune nature of God is not something that can be fully conceptualized in temporal human language. No matter what words we use to express it, it always falls short. But what we can affirm, is that God is an eternal community of three co-existing persons who are "one."

By absorbing our separation through his death, Jesus became, in himself, the bridge between man and God. He did not merely provide a bridge to bring us back into oneness with God, he is himself the bridge. What this means is that Jesus invites us not into a religion, full of rituals and mystical modalities intended to unite us to God through our own determined efforts, but into an inclusive relationship with himself. And it is this relational intimacy between you and Jesus that is, in itself, the portal that brings you back into oneness with God.

And the most remarkable part of this entire story is that God offers this restoration of relational intimacy freely to humanity. We will explore this more in the coming chapters.

HEALING TEACHING

The most common picture of God in the world today is one of an angry being that is obsessed with judging, condemning, and accusing us. In these religious ideas, God is depicted as one who takes joy in our destruction and punishment. But the story of scripture paints a different portrait—one of a God who doesn't simply love us, he likes us. And because he likes us, he longs to be with us. This is the sanctuary theme of the Bible and it permeates the entire narrative from beginning to end.

As beautifully stated by pastor David Asscherick, "God doesn't just love you, he likes you."

REFLECT

In Jesus (fully God and fully man), broken community with God is healed. Through his life he demonstrated the truth of what God is really like. Through his death he took upon himself the full weight of our separation. Through his resurrection he overcame the eternal breaking of oneness with God and each other. Jesus is the solution to the sin problem. He has defeated it in his life, death, and resurrection, and now he invites all who want to be reunited to community with God and others to come to him; he will restore us to relational oneness with himself and, in turn, the fullness of who God is.

CONNECT

Review _____

Open _____

Ask _____

Decide _____

ENGAGE

Scan the QR code to watch this chapter's accompanying Reflection video.

SCAN ME: THE LAMB

6. THE CROSS

So far, the narrative of scripture has unfolded in a simple but confronting story of love, betrayal, and sacrifice. It is a story of Creator, who made us for his love and gave himself completely in order to bring us back to himself. Such a story is unheard of in this world. Virtually every religion has man at the center. The journey is always about what we can do to be reconnected with the divine. But in the Bible, it is the exact opposite. The journey is not about what we have done, can do, or will do. It is about what God himself has done.

But this story, beautiful as it may be, is not without its discomfort. The cross confronts us with one glaring reality, without which we simply cannot appreciate or experience oneness with God—*we are sinners*. And yet, for many of us this is a difficult proposition to embrace. After all, we didn't ask to be here. Why do we have to carry the blame for being sinners when we didn't ask to be sinners? We simply emerged from our mother's womb into this catastrophic and broken universe and are now expected to accept responsibility for it? The entire thing just doesn't seem fair. To make matters worse, beneath the narrative of redemption there seems to be an ugly underlying assumption that goes something like this: "I love you, so I have given my son to die for you. Now believe in him or I will kill you."

Okay, perhaps that is a bit hyperbolic. But the tension is there to some degree. Therefore, what are we to do with it? To begin the journey, let's take a look at the following verses. Compare and contrast the meaning between them.

Romans 5:12-14   Romans 5:15-17

_____   _____

_____   _____

_____   _____

Notice what is happening in these verses. Paul is explaining that, through no fault of your own, sin entered the world and death spread. In other words, Adam's transgression broke the human species. It did something that forever altered our humanness. We were created for eternity, but instead we now live a short conscious existence filled with suffering, and then we expire. It's the tragic outcome of Adam's sin which we inherit. And this was through no fault of our own.

However, something else took place through no fault of our own. Paul goes on to describe how in the same way that death spread to all through Adam's sin, life spreads to all through Jesus. In other words, what Jesus did on the cross restores life to all humanity through no fault of our own. While we were separated from Creator, without a thought for his heart, God came in the person of his son, absorbed our separation, and now life is available to all through no act of our own.

Let's put this in simple language. The narrative of salvation is not God saying, "Accept Jesus or I will kill you." It's God saying, "You are already dead. I want to give you life." In Adam, all of us are dead—his sin separated the human race from the only source of life. So God doesn't have to threaten us with death. We are already in its grasp. But because Jesus absorbed our sin and its collateral effects, we can reclaim the life that is ours to begin with.

The God who Came Down...

To bring this point home, let's explore the cross in a bit more detail. The cross was an instrument of Roman execution. It was used to torture and humiliate criminals and enemies of Rome. While many today wear the cross as an adornment, it was once considered a terrifying object, used by oppressive empires to induce physical and psychological damage on their enemies. Tied and nailed to the cross, one would be left hanging until dead, often by asphyxiation—a process that could last up to three days.

Read and discuss 1 Peter 2:24 and Colossians 1:19–22. What narrative do these verses paint of Jesus, the cross, and the sacrificial lamb from the last chapter?

_____

_____

_____

It is clear that, on the cross, Jesus absorbed the separation and guilt of our sin. Unlike the popular religions of the world, God did not demand we climb up a mountain to earn our redemption. To the contrary, he came down the mountain in the person of Jesus. And it is the God-son Jesus who is, in himself, our redemption. In other words, salvation is not a ritual or a religion. Salvation is a person. Jesus is the lamb who restores everything.

Recall, in the previous chapter, we explored how a lamb was brought to the sanctuary and the sinner would confess his sin over it, "transferring" his guilt onto the innocent creature to be slain in his/her place. This is precisely what Jesus did for us. To understand this more, let's explore the closing scenes of his life.

Read and discuss the story as it unfolds in Luke 22:39–45; Matthew 26:47–53; Mark 15:16–32; and John 19:28–30.

_____
_____
_____

Notice that in Luke's account, Jesus appears to be suffering before the cross. The capillaries under his skin are bursting. The stress he is under is almost too much for his human body to bear. He is bleeding and no one has even touched him yet. Something beyond physical is crushing him.

Then, in his hour of greatest need, Matthew tells us his disciples abandon him and Judas betrays him. After being falsely accused, Mark says he was mocked, whipped, and, finally, crucified. This all took place in the first three hours of his crucifixion. But then something strange happens. The story goes silent. While the first three hours of his ordeal are recorded in detail, there is no record of the last three. Nothing more is said of his time on the cross until he nears his death at the end of six hours. Matthew writes: "Now from the sixth hour there was darkness over all the land until the ninth hour. About the ninth hour Jesus cried with a loud voice, saying, 'Eli, Eli, lama sabachthani?' That is, 'My God, my God, why have you forsaken me?'" (Matthew 27:45–46)

In order to comprehend the depth of what is happening here, we need to remember everything we have discovered in the story of scripture so far. Jesus is God, and has always existed in eternal community with the Father and the Spirit. And yet now he feels separated. As the guilt of the world is placed on him, he is plunged into the separation that sin causes between us and God. The Aramaic term "sabachthani," which Jesus uses, means "to be left alone." On the cross, Jesus inhales the opposite of creation's shabbat. In our place, he plunges into the depths of "shebaq."

SHABBAT
Rest, Oneness

SHEBAQ
Alone, Separation

The separation that God wants to heal could only be bridged one way—Jesus must absorb our brokenness and be separated on our behalf, so that, by faith, in his sacrifice, we can be brought back into oneness with the Father. Jesus takes our guilt, our shame, and mysteriously grafts it into his own being. He stands in our place and becomes sin for us. The separation is so intense that Jesus, in his humanity, feels as though the sanctuary nature of God has been shattered—eternal community forever fractured.

Read and discuss Isaiah 59:2, 53:4–5, 12; and 2 Corinthians 5:21.
How do these verses help us understand what Jesus is going through?

_____
_____
_____

Only six hours after he was lifted up on the cross, John tells us that Jesus breathed his final breath and collapsed. His final words were, "It is finished." The plan of salvation, formulated before the world began and revealed through the sanctuary, had been accomplished. The separation between God and humanity had come to an end.

After Jesus died, John says, "one of the soldiers pierced his side with a spear, and immediately blood and water came out" (John 19:34). What does this mean?

Two things: first, Jesus was clearly dead; second, something else beside the cross must have killed Jesus. No one died on the cross after only six hours. It was a slow method of execution. And although there is no conclusive answer, some commentators have proposed evidence of heart rupture. In other words, the spiritual anguish of our guilt was so overwhelming that Jesus's heart may have literally burst. Separation had claimed its prize.

However, the story doesn't end there. In order for salvation to be complete, something else needed to happen.

Read Matthew 28:1–10 and Romans 4:25. Summarize here:

_____
_____
_____

The resurrection of Jesus is so central to humanity's salvation story that the New Testament authors considered the entire narrative pointless without it. But why?

Think of it this way. When humanity fell, we entered into a state of relational separation from God. This relational separation ultimately led to a state of permanent detachment from reality, that is, death. Death is separation's ultimate weapon—its prime tool. Death manifests the exact opposite of what a god of "withness" desires. It manifests irreversible and eternal separateness.

We will explore the biblical theme of death and eternity in more detail in part 3 of our journey, but for now consider this: when Jesus conquered death he reversed, in himself, the very thing that threatens to separate us permanently from God. What this means is that, in Jesus, something remarkable has taken place: separation has been conquered, death has been reversed, a way out has been discovered and secured in Jesus. Because of this, separation no longer has to be the fate or destiny of the human species. We can now, through Jesus, be restored not merely to oneness with God, but to eternal oneness with him.

Read the following verses and share what they mean to you:
1 Corinthians 15:54–55, Hosea 13:14, Revelation 1:18, 2 Timothy 1:10, Isaiah 25:8

REFLECT

The cross was an instrument of execution for criminals. On it, Jesus gave his life to restore our broken community with God and one another. But it was not the cross that killed him. It was the weight of our separation. After his burial, his disciples were disillusioned and confused. But three days later, he rose from the dead, and today he says to us, "I am the first and the last, and the living One; and I was dead, and behold, I am alive forevermore, and I have the keys of death…" (Revelation 1:17–18). Because he has conquered sin and death, Jesus has become the eternal champion of divine-human oneness. He has crushed sin and separation forever, and he offers this restoration to us as a gift.

CONNECT

Review _____

_____

Open _____

_____

Ask _____

_____

Decide _____

_____

ENGAGE

Scan the QR code to watch this chapter's accompanying Reflection video.

SCAN ME: THE CROSS

7. THE GIFT

The story of scripture is about God. It reveals his heart to us in amazing ways. In it we discover how deeply he loves and how he is willing to go to any length to restore us to intimacy with himself. In Jesus, we also encounter God doing for us what we could not do for ourselves—healing the separation sin has caused. This gift is so good and so free that many struggle to believe it can be true. Two questions naturally arise. First, isn't there something I'm supposed to do to earn God's approval? Second, how does this gift of salvation translate to the social, political, and interpersonal brokenness of our present world?

These two questions are extremely personal, and this is exactly what God intends. Because God is love, created us for relationship, and likes to "sanctuary" with us, he has not revealed himself in a philosophical way but in a personal way. When he made us from the dust of the ground with his own hands, when he "sabbathed" with Adam and Eve in their first full day of life, when he sent prophets to speak to his people, when he came himself in the very person of Jesus, God demonstrated that he is active in our time and space. He is more than simply "there." He is actually "with."

This means God's salvation story is more than an ethereal formula that guarantees eternal life. It is a historical reality that impacts and transforms who we are and how we relate to our neighbors, societies, and even enemies. Salvation, then, is not a legal loophole or ticket to a future pie in the sky. It is an experience in the here and now—a process that seeks to restore in our broken psyches the other-centered design of God's heart. And the good news that undergirds this experience is the beautifully ludicrous promise that the entire thing is free. There is no religious code, moral list, or ritual portal through which we attain the right to enter into this experience. To the contrary, it is a gift of forgiveness and rebirth offered to everyone and experienced by anyone who embraces it.

Isn't there Something I'm Supposed to do to Be Saved?

When we are confronted with Jesus's sacrifice for us, how he took our guilt and separation so we could be set free, the natural human response is: "It cannot possibly be this easy." This is a normal reaction. After all, everything we receive in life, from an allowance, to our degrees and promotions—all of it is earned by hard work and the endless pursuit of proving ourselves. But when it comes to salvation, it's the opposite.

To begin exploring this question, read the following texts: Romans 8:7, 1 Corinthians 2:14, Romans 3:10–11, John 6:44, Ezekiel 34:11, 16, and 1 John 5:12. What do these verses say about experiencing salvation?

_____
_____
_____

One thing is clear: Mankind is so absorbed by the power of sin that we are helplessly trapped in its web. Left to ourselves, we would never even notice. But God, in his great love, has come searching for us. And if it were not for God pursuing us relentlessly, no one would ever turn to him. The very fact that you are reading this is evidence, not of your deep spirituality, but of his radical pursuit of you. He is already chasing you, and your heart is beginning to respond.

Read the text below and answer the following question: How are humans saved?

"For by grace you have been saved through faith; and that not of yourselves, it is the gift of God; not of works, that no one would boast" (Ephesians 2:8–9).

_____
_____
_____

If you answered, "grace through faith," congratulations! You got it right. We are

χάρις - charis

Grace comes from the Greek word "charis" which means "favor". To receive grace is to receive a favor.

πίστις - pistis

Faith comes from the Greek word "pistis" which means "trust". To have faith in God means to put our trust in him.

not saved by our moral acts or by how ethical we are, but, by "grace through faith." But what exactly does "grace through faith" mean?

Picture it this way. Suppose you are in the middle of the ocean. There is no land anywhere in sight. You can swim all you want, but you are too far out. All of your swimming will amount to nothing. You need to be rescued. Thankfully, a helicopter appears out of nowhere and tosses a line to you. Your only job is to take hold of the line so you can be pulled out of the water and taken to safety. That line is grace. By placing your trust in the line, you are exercising faith. The line is what saves you. Faith is what enables you to grab the line. And that is how salvation works. Grace is what saves us. Faith is what enables us to take hold of grace. God seeks us, finds us, and draws us to himself. He then offers us the gift of salvation. But it is up to us to embrace it. This is why, when asked "What must I do to be saved?", Jesus's followers replied, "believe (*pistis*) in the Lord Jesus Christ, and you will be saved..." (Acts 16:31).

> *When we choose to put our trust in Jesus Christ, three things happen at the same time. Find out what in the following texts: John 16:8; Romans 2:4; and Romans 12:3.*

_____
_____
_____

Notice how all of these are gifts of God. A person cannot be saved without first admitting they are a sinner. So, God sends his Holy Spirit, as a gift, to show us our sin. Likewise, a person cannot be saved unless they turn away from their sin (repentance). And it is by his kindness that God draws us away from sin and toward himself. And finally, by faith we believe that our sin is pardoned and our guilt is washed away. But we can't manufacture that faith. God gives it to everyone as a gift. In short, the three steps to salvation—confession, repentance, and faith—are all gifts of God. It's as if he just desperately wants to be re-united with us. God has removed every obstacle and impediment. He has provided everything needed for your salvation. There is nothing left for you to do except this one thing: *respond*. While God offers you the free gift of salvation, he won't force it onto you. The choice is yours alone.

How Does this Gift Translate to the Injustices of Our World?

Not only is salvation a free gift to receive, it is also a free gift to retain. Salvation is not like a zero-down deal at the local auto lot. You don't take it home, "free today," and start your "good behavior" payments later on. If this were the case, it wouldn't be a gift. A gift, by definition, is always free.

But this raises a pertinent issue. If salvation is such a free gift, then won't this lead people into passivity? A kind of state of mind where we ignore the suffering around us because doing good things doesn't get us to heaven, and we are already assured that we are getting in? Or even worse, can't this "free" gift of salvation be used to justify our own participation in and perpetuation of societal ills such as nationalism, sexism, or racism? After all, if we have guaranteed access to heaven, then what's the point of confronting these very real injustices in our churches and neighborhoods?

To answer this question, go to Ephesians 2. Read verses 8–9 as a warm-up and then zoom in on verse 10.

_____
_____
_____

In this verse, Paul says "we are God's handiwork." In the Greek, the word "handiwork" is *poiēma,* which means "a work." Interestingly, *poiēma* is the word from which we derive the English word "poem." When a poet writes a poem, he works it until it is beautiful. In the same way, the saved are God's poem. He doesn't leave us as he found us. Instead, he works in us and through us until he arrives at something beautiful. So, not only does God forgive our sins—he transforms our lives.

Paul says we were "created in Christ Jesus for good works" (Ephesians 2:10). God never intended to just forgive us. He had much more in mind than that. God intended that through Jesus we would be restored to harmony with the law of love.

When you place your faith in Jesus, you enter into a transformational experience in which he metamorphose you into a brand new creation with a new heart, in restored harmony with God's heart of love. This divine-human synchronicity is simply the natural outworking of being put back into harmony with God's heart. And it is via this restored relational oneness that God is now gathering a new humanity that will populate a new society—a civilization that moves, not according to the narratives of power, coercion, consumerism or self-advancement, but to the rhythms of other-centered love. A humanity defined, not by political philosophies or coercive governmental structures, but by the way of Jesus.

It is to this new humanity that we now turn.

HEALING TEACHING

Spiritually abusive communities often burden their members with an endless list of behavioural and performative tasks. In some, moral perfection is even demanded. These teachings cause emotional and psychological damage and can lead to anxiety disorders, OCD, and depression. But in Jesus, the story is liberating. He has met all the requirements of eternity on our behalf and there is nothing for us to add. He is our perfection. The gospel then, is not an invitation to a new religion. It is the end of religion and the invitation to something infinitely better: an unhindered relationship with Creator that heals us, frees us, and transforms us.

REFLECT

In Jesus, we have a new beginning. God heals our hearts so that we come to love what he loves and hate what he hates. This journey is one that will take the rest of our lives. We will never be flawless in this world, but we have the promise that God will never turn his back on us. As we daily walk with Jesus, God transforms us into his other-centered, agape-love image (the opposite of our self-centered empires). We go from living lives out of harmony with love, to lives lived for God and others. In short, believers do not manifest a good life in order to be accepted. Believers do so because they have already been accepted. This radical acceptance is the thing that re-harmonizes us with the heart of Creator. We become God's poem, his work of art. And in the end, it is through this poem that God will birth a new humanity, marked by true compassion, cosmic justice, and eternal oneness.

CONNECT

Review _____

Open _____

Ask _____

Decide _____

ENGAGE

Scan the QR code to watch this chapter's accompanying Reflection video.

SCAN ME: THE GIFT

8. THE RESTORATION

The narrative of scripture does not isolate itself to text. Instead, it insists on entering and altering the human experience. This means the story of the Bible is more than just a chronicle to be cognitively or vocally rehearsed. It is, in its fullest sense, a story to be lived. As a result, we cannot fully enter into its plot line without allowing it to rewrite our personal stories. This "re-authoring" includes a transformation of our values and world views, but also something significantly deeper and more meaningful.

Think of it like this. Imagine you are gifted a rundown house, so you hire a project manager to renovate it. Three months later, you come back and the house looks amazing. It has a new roof, walls, and floors. The entire layout has been modernized and stylized to your liking. But when you try to turn on your lights you discover your house is not connected to the grid. You try to have a bath and discover that your house has no plumbing system either. At this point you are beyond furious, so you call the project manager to find out what happened.

"We only fixed what you can see," he says. "We left all the other stuff alone."

How angry would you be?

Here's the point: God is not interested in simply renewing the surface of our lives. He wants to go beneath the surface. He wants to step into the underground of our psyches, the places no one can see, and bring healing and renewal to that dimension of us. And it is through this inner rebirth that the new humanity of Jesus becomes more than a teaching, but a lived experience.

But what exactly is this process like? And why does it matter? These are the two questions we will explore in this chapter.

What is this Process Like?

Recall how the story began. God is love. He does not exist for his own personal gain, which is why John could say, "God so loved the world that he gave..." (John 3:16). This other-centered way of living formed the basis for God's creation. Both natural and moral law reveal it. The trees receive carbon dioxide and give it back as oxygen. The clouds receive condensation and give it back as rain. Rivers give to the sea and the sea returns to the rivers. Any time this pattern is broken, death ensues.

This is precisely what took place at the fall. Adam and Eve were created to receive love from God. It was like a river flowing from the heart of Creator into the heart of humanity. Then, as all rivers do, the flow would continue outward toward others, the earth, and its creatures. With this flow in motion, the terrestrial ecosystem would thrive from generation to generation. There would be no empires, no resource control, no war, exploitation, or lack. Society would be organized, not around governmental laws enforced by threat of punishment, but around a mutually collaborative spirit of adventure and connection, all enhanced by the infinite fountain of divine love coursing through us.

But when sin entered the story, it caused a mysterious rift, or separation, between man and Creator. The flow of love was interrupted.

From this moment onward, the story introduces us to interpersonal tension, lies, blame, and discord.

Empires are born, wars are fought, families are splintered.

The spirit of mutual collaboration is replaced by patriarchy, tribalism, humanitarian injustice, and the endless cycles of ancestral and generational trauma.

As our journey moves forward, we will circle back around to some of the broader themes of injustice. (And yes, we will even look at how Christianity has contributed to so much pain in the world!) But for now, lets focus on the way in which these cycles generate spiritual and psychological wounds.

Because, it turns out, the good news of the Jesus-way is that, in him, we can experience a transformational encounter that heals and restores us despite our traumas. And this healing is the real beauty of the gospel.

Far beyond a new belief system or a new way of seeing the world, the promise of Jesus is that he offers us a new way to be human, a new way to inhabit our bodies, and a new way to exist in the world. This new way is a foretaste, in the here and now, of what eternity, and the new reconstructed neighborhood of Jesus, will be like.

To keep things simple, we are going to break this whole transformational experience thing into three overarching headings: The Upward, Inward, and Outward Life.

The Upward Life

Throughout scripture, God repeatedly invites humanity toward a centered and exclusive relationship with himself. In Jeremiah 30:22, he says, "you will be my people, and I will be your God." And in Exodus 20:3, he says, "You must not have any other god but me." This invitation to put God first in our lives is the call to the upward life.

Some have wondered if these texts show an egotistical and jealous being who wants to control his creatures by demanding blind allegiance. However, these texts are more accurately understood when we consider the context in which they were written.

Now of course, that context is very big, so to keep things simple we are going to focus on one story—the story of Israel.

The nation of Israel is central to the Biblical worldview. But the nation itself has an origin story that begins with a man named Jacob. Read Genesis 25:21-23. How does God identify the babies in Rebekah's womb?

_____
_____
_____

Notice that God calls them both nations. Esau would eventually become the father of the Edomite nation. And Jacob would become the father of the nation of Israel. However, things got complicated once Jacob was born. Read Genesis 25:24-26 and answer this question: Why was Jacob given that name? What does it mean?

_____
_____
_____

The Hebrew name "Jacob" literally means "supplanter" or "deceiver." It basically describes a person who uses cunning to get their way. Today we would think of this as a conman or a scammer.

But why would a family give their child such a name? You have to read the rest of the story (Genesis 25-33) to get the full picture. But the simplest answer is that Jacob belonged to a family of con-artists. His mother and his uncle were both sneaky liars as was his father Isaac. Jacob's name (deceiver) said a lot more about them than it did about him.

Nevertheless, with this false identity forced onto him, Jacob goes on to repeat the toxic cycles of his family. He becomes just what others said he was—a scammer who cheated to get his own way. Throughout the story he con's his brother and uncle, but worst of all—he cheats his own blind and aging father.

Toward the end of his story, however, something remarkable happens. Read Genesis 32: 22-32. What does God say to him in verse 28?

_____

_____

_____

God changes Jacob's name to Israel. From "deceiver" to "overcomer." However, recall Genesis 25: 21-23. Who did God say Jacob was before he was even born?

_____

_____

_____

Here is the main point: Before Jacob was born, he was Israel. "Jacob" was a false identity given to him by the people around him. But his true identity was never Jacob. It was always Israel. This means that in Genesis 32 God is not giving Jacob a new identity so much as he is restoring Jacob to his true identity—who he was always meant to be.

Likewise, due to the power of sin and the cycles of trauma and pain we inherit as we enter this broken world, each of us has been raised in environments that fuel a false identity. We are told lies about who we are by social media, corporations, and even family. These lies eventually form our identity and we struggle to see who we really are. We buy into them and begin to live them out, perpetuating cycles of dysfunction and drama in our lives. But here is the good news: Jesus came to liberate us from the false gods who lie to us, the false self we have bought into, and restore us to who God always intended us to be: conquerors, overcomers, and friends.

When God invites us to have no other gods before him, he is not being egocentric. To the contrary, he is manifesting his authentic other-centeredness. He knows that when we put him first by turning away from the gods who lie to us, he can then step inside and bring truth to the deepest, most exiled parts of us.

Think of it like this: God knows that our self-image is broken and wounded. And he knows that what we need in order to fully heal is to experience truth—one that is based not on flawed human beings or mere escapes from our pain, but on the never-changing, ever-present, agape-love Creator of our being.

In other words, God wants to replace all of our false gods with himself.

He wants to be our new identity.

He wants to be our new truth.

And through this relationship, he wants to move us from the prison house of fear, dismissiveness, and self-protection to the green pastures of security, inner peace, and divine-human interconnectedness.

The Inward Life

Jacob's journey was not easy. The story of his fight with God ends by saying he limped for the rest of his life. This limp demonstrates that an encounter with the divine will leave us forever changed because the God of scripture is not an energy to be used to achieve our vision board, but a conscious being who will step on our toes and rattle our world in order to awaken us to healing truth.

In the Upward dimension, God invites us to be his as he longs to be ours. In the Inward dimension, he invites us to do something more: *to let him in*. To open the closet of our despairs and allow his grace to fill, to cleanse, and to restore. This experience demands raw honesty between us and God. Depending on the complexity of your journey, a counselor or therapist may be a wonderful companion to unravel the knots with. Whatever it looks like, know this: following Jesus isn't merely about having a new set of propositional ideas called "beliefs." It's about letting him into the fullness of who you are and experiencing his compassion in the darkest corners of your world.

The Outward Life

The Outward life is the final bracket we will explore. This one deals more with what a new life in Jesus looks like once the Upward and Inward dimensions have been flooded with his grace. And, to be honest, its really quite simple! The ancient king, Solomon, put it best when he wrote, "Above all else, guard your heart, for everything you do flows from it" (Proverbs 4:23).

In other words, when your heart is in tune with God your true identity begins to emerge and the healing journey goes from a personal experience to one that changes the environment you inhabit. This is what Jesus meant when he said, "Streams of living water will flow from within" (John 7:38).

*Read and meditate on the following texts in scripture.
What new horizons do they open up for your healing journey?*

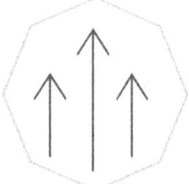 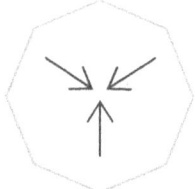 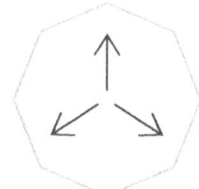

The Upward Life	The Inward Life	The Outward Life
Matthew 6:33	Psalm 139:13–14	1 Corinthians 13:1–13
Psalm 63:1–8, 100	Psalm 139: 23-24	2 Corinthians 5:17
Proverbs 16:3	Revelation 3:20	Romans 12:2

Why Does this Matter?

Some may wonder, why? Why does God step into these areas of our lives? In fact, some of you might be asking why this chapter has detoured from our scriptural road trip to explore these personal issues. But this is a mistake. The present chapter has not deviated from the narrative. It is fully immersed in it because you and I are characters in the story. It's one thing for us to explore the story of God from afar, but the God of the Bible comes close and invites us to enter the story.

We must also remember that, ultimately, the story of scripture is not about *us*. It's about him. In scripture, we discover God's desire to "sanctuary" with us. We are introduced to a sanctuary in heaven (Hebrews 9:24) that represents God's eternal desire to dwell with us. This desire is then communicated through the earthly sanctuary that God instructed the Israelites to build. (Exodus 25:8–9) In the New Testament, the earthly sanctuary building meets its end in Jesus. With the separation between God and man healed, God no longer uses a building to communicate his love. Now he uses something much more powerful and effective.

Read 1 Corinthians 3:16–17, 6:19–20 and 2 Corinthians 6:16 to find out what the new sanctuary on earth is.

_____

_____

_____

There is still a sanctuary on earth that communicates the narrative of heaven's sanctuary: *us*.

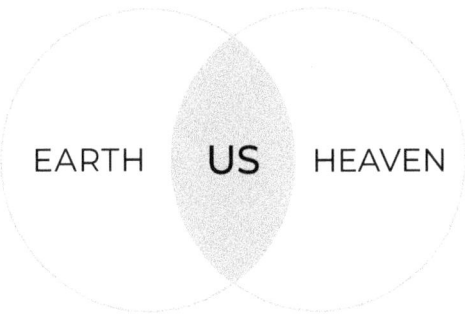

You and I are now the place where people can encounter the beauty of God. If God were to restore us halfway—by giving us a new religion or worldview—without actually changing the uncomfortable things underneath, we would not be able to manifest his love. Others would encounter us and see us claiming to be his people, but still living out selfish, toxic, and unhealthy cycles. When we allow God to transform those deep areas of our lives, we are allowing God to liberate us from our negative cycles and, in turn, manifest a life of enthusiasm, purpose, and counter-cultural beauty.

This way of being is the way of Jesus, by which we—hurting and imperfect people—become "little sanctuaries" in which the Spirit of the divine dwells. And while we won't be perfect this side of heaven, we are nevertheless invited to become living, breathing temples where others can experience the beauty of God's presence.

And here's the best part: as we each dance with God in this divine, human transformation, we begin to experience oneness with him and each other. The end result is a new civilization, a new society, and a reconstructed neighborhood in which each person moves and flows to the rhythm of other-centered love. And it is through this new humanity that the Bible teaches that God will rebirth a new world and a new story that will never end.

In short, the gospel is not merely good news about going to heaven; the gospel is good news about every facet of our humanity. And it starts right here, right now.

HEALING TEACHING

As good as the salvation story is, it has been misused by systems of oppression throughout history. For example, many slave owners in America were big believers in salvation as a free gift that gets us to heaven free of charge. However, the story of scripture is about much more than a free ride to heaven. While salvation is a free gift, it manifests as a life of authentic compassion and justice. To claim grace as a veil for abuse and exploitation is a contradiction of what grace is and does. Salvation is not me leaving earth and going to heaven because I said the right prayer. Salvation is heaven coming down and living in me, right here right now, transforming my relationship to myself, my neighbours, and the ecosystem that I belong to. And it starts today!

REFLECT

Focusing on how God restores us personally is not an add-on to the story of scripture—it is the natural outflow of its plotline. God originally created reality to operate according to the law of love. Sin broke that design. God is now restoring all things back to the original pattern, and he invites each of us to trust him by opening our lives to his redemptive plan. When we do, he aims to renew more than just our beliefs; rather, he aims to renew even the nitty-gritty details of our lives, for it is in the everyday details that his love shines most fully. As we allow his grace to wash over our brokenness and transform even these private corners of our being, he promises to shine through us so that others can encounter his healing love.

CONNECT

Review _____
_____
_____

Open _____
_____
_____

Ask _____
_____
_____

Decide _____
_____
_____

ENGAGE

Scan the QR code to watch this chapter's accompanying Reflection video.

SCAN ME: THE RESTORATION

9. THE FAMILY

Salvation is a gift. Jesus secured our healing and now offers each of us the eternal benefits of his death and resurrection. However, being a Jesus follower is far from an individual thing. When we are saved, we are given a new identity and become a part of something bigger than ourselves. Salvation isn't just about my forgiveness. It's also about entering into God's story and becoming a part of what he is doing in the world.

After the fall, God put into action the plan of salvation, which had been formulated before the creation of the world. That plan was fully completed at the cross, but the story is not over. God is now working to apply his salvation to all people, with the goal of restoring the world back to its original design. As believers, we are called to be part of that restoration.

But we are getting ahead of ourselves. There are two questions we need to explore to bring these different pieces together. The first is, how is God bringing his salvation story to all people? And the second is, what is our role in all of this?

How is God Bringing His Salvation Story to all People?

Read 1 Corinthians 15:45–49. Fill in the description of the first Adam and then go through the text again and do the same for the second, or "last," Adam. Who is this second Adam?

FIRST ADAM _____
_____
_____

_____ LAST ADAM
_____
_____

The first Adam is the Adam we encounter in the book of Genesis. He is the father of the human race. He became a "living soul," is "natural," and from the "earth." By contrast, the second Adam is referred to as a "life-giver," is "spiritual," and from "heaven." There is only one person in all of scripture who came from heaven, was spiritual, and a life-giver—God himself, Jesus. The first Adam is Adam. The second Adam is Jesus. Paul finished this message with the promise that just as all those who are children of Adam are like him (out of harmony), all those who are children of Jesus will also be like him (in harmony).

But why does this matter? Simple. All humans born under the first Adam belong to the family of Earth. All humans born again under the second Adam (Christ) belong to the family of heaven. So, Jesus is the new head of humanity for all who accept him. This means that there are two families now. Those whose ancestor is Adam, and those whose ancestor is Christ. Paul explains this a bit more in the following text:

But when the fullness of the time came, God sent out his Son, born to a woman, born under the law, that he might redeem those who were under the law, that we might receive the adoption as children. And because you are children, God sent out the Spirit of his Son into your hearts, crying, "Abba, Father!" So you are no longer a bondservant, but a son; and if a son, then an heir of God through Christ (Galatians 4:4–7).

In Paul's time, when a person was adopted into a family they assumed the same identity as the family. This means that an adopted son was not regarded as an adopted son. He was regarded as a natural born son. His old identity was canceled out. He was no longer who he once was. Any debts or obligations from his former life were removed. Any heritage, legacy, or social status from his former family were also erased. He now had an entirely new identity under the new father of the house. As believers, we have been reborn under the last Adam (Jesus) and adopted into God's family. We no longer belong to the first Adam. We now have a new identity. This means that everything we were under the first Adam, our shame; regrets; and traumas, have been erased. We now have an entirely new identity defined by the character of Jesus. He is our new attachment. With him, we are no longer defined by who we were, but who he is.

Read Ephesians 2:19–22. What is this new family of God?

_____
_____
_____

This family Paul is referring to is what the New Testament calls the "church." In the New Testament, "church" is never referred to as a literal building. Instead, it is a community of believers who do life together. In fact, the original Greek word for church is "*ecclesia,*" which literally means "group of people." And it is through this group of people that God is bringing his salvation story to the whole world.

Where Do I Fit Into this Story?

The gospel of Jesus is not simply a story of God's love for us. It is a complete rebirth from our Adamic humanity to the new humanity of Jesus. To borrow from author Ty Gibson, Jesus is the father of Humanity 2.0. Those who remain under Adam 1.0 are destined to perpetuate his legacy of broken attachments. But those who receive Adam 2.0 (Jesus) as their new ancestor enter into a new dimension of harmonic attachment with Creator. And because that transition is such an intense experience, God has gathered this new family of his into what he calls the "church." This church is the means through which God reaches out and impacts the world with healing love. Hence, in the Bible it is called the "body of Christ"—his hands and feet reaching out to a lost and broken humanity with a story of hope and rebirth.

How do we become a part of this family? Jesus gave his followers a ritual to celebrate as they joined themselves to his church. Read Matthew 28:18–19, Galatians 3:27, and Acts 2:36–41.

The word "baptism" literally means "to immerse." When we are baptized, we are immersed in water as a public declaration that we now belong to God and his new family. However, baptism means something more. To find out, read Romans 6:4.

Do not miss the depth of what Paul is saying here. In baptism, we identify with the death, burial, and resurrection of Jesus. It is, in a sense, the most intimate and romantic ritual a person could ever go through. When you are lowered into the water you are identifying yourself with the death and burial of Jesus. You are dying to your old self. Your life in Adam is being buried. Your old identity washed away. You, as you know you, dies with Jesus. This is profound. Baptism is not just a bath. In fact, there is nothing magical about the water. It is the chance to re-enact and identify yourself with Jesus's death and burial for you—that is powerful.

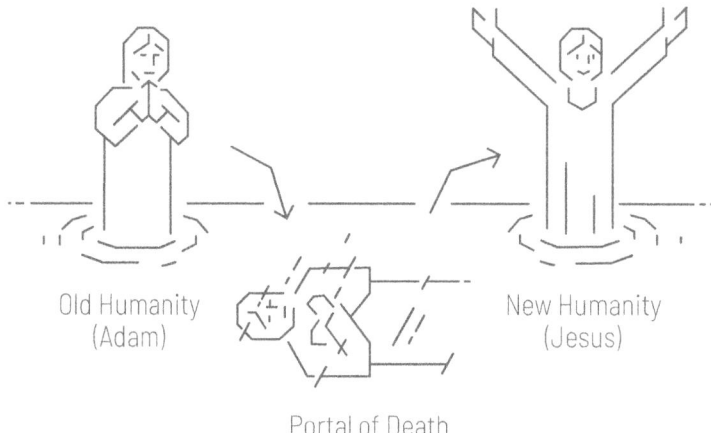

Old Humanity (Adam)

New Humanity (Jesus)

Portal of Death

Baptism is yet another evidence of God's love and desire to sanctuary with us. Through baptism, God allows us to experience, in our time and space, something that has taken place in heaven's sanctuary—the forgiveness of our sins and adoption into his new family. Thus, in baptism we celebrate the reality of our new identity as his adopted children. And finally, as we are raised out of the water we are raised to new life in Jesus—identifying with his resurrection, we emerge a new creation with a new identity. "The old things have passed away. Behold, all things have become new" (2 Corinthians 5:17).

However, don't miss the uncomfortable element here. According to this story, new life is reserved for those who pass through the portal of self-death. Death to self, then, is the passageway to rebirth. And this death to self is celebrated in the ritual of baptism. Through it we become a part of Jesus's church and are adopted from our old humanity in Adam into his new, restored humanity.

Read Matthew 9:9–12, 28:16–20; Acts 1:8; and Romans 10:14–15. What do these texts say about entering God's story?

When we are saved, God adopts us and gives us a new identity. Our old life is washed away and a new life begins. This new life is defined not by the legacy of the old life (addictions, broken attachments, regrets, etc.), but by the legacy of Jesus (victorious, connected, free).

This doesn't mean Jesus followers are perfect; we still have tons of issues to work through. This transformation journey is also a process, more like a walk and not a sprint. And yet, as we do this walk with God and, day by day, learn to trust his voice over the lies that have enslaved us, we experience a whole new dimension of being.

And what better way to do this than in community, with others who are likewise celebrating this new humanity? As we join ourselves to this new family, Jesus invites us to celebrate the ritual of baptism. By being immersed in water, we publicly announce our new identity as a child of God and identify ourselves with his death, burial, and resurrection. From that day on we are part of the *ecclesia* (church/ community) of God, and the mission of the *ecclesia* becomes our own.

REFLECT

Thinking back to the very start of the lessons, we have come full circle. From creation, to catastrophe, and now—thanks to Jesus—a recreation back to God's original design. He is now gathering his family—all who choose to love and be aligned to his design—and invites all within it, you and me, to be a part of growing that family. There is only one thing left to do, and that is for you to make the decision to embrace all of him. The apostle Peter said it best,

> *"Now why do you wait? Arise, be baptized, and wash away your sins, calling on his name." (Acts 22:16)*

CONNECT

Review _____

_____

Open _____

_____

Ask _____

_____

Decide _____

_____

ENGAGE

Scan the QR code to watch this chapter's accompanying Reflection video.

SCAN ME: THE FAMILY

PIT STOP

Congratulations on finishing part one! By now, you will have learned the overarching story of the Bible, from God/Creation to Restoration. In part two, we are going to dive deeper, and explore the narrative of Empire and its place in our cosmic struggle. The battle between good and evil didn't end when Jesus died on the cross. It continues and, in many ways, intensifies into a planetary struggle in which God, Jesus came to reveal, is cleverly replaced by a deceptive counter-god and counter-narrative. As we explore this part of the story, you are going to encounter suspense, intrigue, and twists you didn't expect. In the end, you will see with greater clarity what your purpose is today at both the local and cosmic level.

But before we get into that, we need to make sure that the foundation is set because none of what we will explore in the future makes any sense if you don't have a good baseline! So, think of this chapter as a pit stop on your road trip toward the heart of God. The purpose of this pit stop is to go back to the beginning to "Refresh," "Refine," and "Reinforce" what we have discovered. Use the instructions below and discuss the points with your fellow travelers. By the end of this pit stop you should have a solid foundation for the rest of the journey.

SCAN ME: PART 1 PITSTOP

REFRESH

The Beginning

God is love. He is three in one—an eternal, self-existent community. He did not create because he was needy. He created out of the overflow of his communal love. Mankind was made in his image—the image of love—for the express purpose of living forever in selfless love with one another and with him. In all of this we discover why we exist: *to love and be loved for all eternity.*

The Song

God's love was the foundation for creating a perfect world. Adam and Eve, the first relationship, were designed to make a beautiful world, as co-rulers. This pattern was to repeat each week, leading to the seventh day, Sabbath, which God set aside as a special day of rest for humanity to come celebrate their relationship with him as creator and God. All of this points to God's heart of love, but it also points to God's original design.

The Fall

Sin is the opposite of love. By joining the Satan in his defection, our first parents chose life apart from God. In doing so, they introduced a spiritual vacuum into God's perfect creation. This vacuum of sin caused a spiritual separation between man and God. Because God is the source of all that is good, the separation is the cause of all the suffering in this world. God did not create sin, but because God is love, he created us with the freedom of choice. We can choose either life with God or life apart from God.

The Book

Because of the separation caused by sin, God could no longer dwell with man because his very presence would overwhelm us. In order to be reconnected to us, he would have to draw us back to himself and heal the separation. One way in which he does this is by revealing himself through the Bible. Through it, God leads us, little by little, toward himself, healing our spiritual sin-vacuum so that one day we can be reunited face-to-face.

The Lamb

In Jesus, broken community with God is restored. Throughout his life he demonstrated the truth of what God is really like. Through his death, he took upon himself all of our guilt and shame and buried them. Through his resurrection he overcame the eternal breaking of oneness with God and each other. Jesus is the solution to the broken design. Our only role is to place our trust in him, and when we do he restores us to harmony with heaven and the way of love.

The Cross

The cross was an instrument of execution for criminals. On it, Jesus gave his life to restore our broken community with God and one another. But it was not the cross that killed him. It was the weight of our separation. After his burial, his disciples were disillusioned and confused. But three days later he rose from the dead. Because he has conquered sin and death, Jesus has the right to promise all who love him complete freedom and eternal life.

The Gift

In Jesus, our sins are forgiven and we are declared holy. God heals our hearts so that we come to love what he loves and hate what he hates. This journey is one that will take the rest of our life. We will never be flawless in this world, but we have the promise that God will never turn his back on us. As we daily walk with Jesus, God transforms us into his other-centered, agape-love image (the opposite of our self-centered nature). We go from being self-centered beings to living life for God and others, in harmony with God's law of agape love. We are God's poem, his beautiful work of art.

The Restoration

Focusing on how God restores us personally is not an add-on to the story of scripture—it is the natural outflow of its narrative. God originally created reality to operate according to the law of love. Sin broke that design. God is now restoring all things back to the original pattern, and he invites each of us to trust him by surrendering our lives to his redemption plan. When we do, he aims to renew more than just our beliefs; rather, he aims to renew even the small details of our lives—for it is in the everyday details that his love shines most fully. As we allow his grace to wash over our brokenness and transform even these private corners of our lives, he promises to shine through us so that others can find in us the beauty of his love for them.

The Family

When we are saved, God adopts us and gives us a new identity. Our old life is washed away and a new life begins. This new life is defined not by the legacy of the old life (addictions, sins, toxic cycles, etc.), but by the legacy of Jesus (victorious, selfless, free). By being immersed in water (baptism) we publicly announce our new identity as a child of God and identify ourselves with his death, burial, and resurrection. From that day on we are part of the *ecclesia* (church/community) of God, and the mission of the *ecclesia* becomes our own.

REFINE

The Beginning	*Who is God? What is the Trinity? Why did he create us? How can we understand God's love?* *(Hint: 3 Kinds of Love in the Bible)*
The Song	*What was God's creation like? What law is it built on? What is humanity's purpose?* *(Hint: Think Purpose, Community, Celebration)*
The Fall	*What is the fall? How did it affect creation? How does it help us understand suffering? How does it help us understand God's heart?*
The Book	*What is the purpose of the Bible? How does it help connect us to God? Why can't we enter into God's presence? (Hint: The Sanctuary)*
The Lamb	*What does the Lamb in the Bible represent? How can human beings find redemption? What is sin? How does Jesus save us?*
The Cross	*How deep is Jesus's sacrifice?* *What does the cross say about God's heart? What significance is there in Jesus's resurrection?*
The Gift	*What do you have to do to be saved? Why do believers keep God's law? How are we changed into the image of love?*
The Restoration	*What does it mean to be restored by God's grace? What areas of our lives does God step into? (Hint: Upward, Inward, and Outward)*
The Family	*Who are the first and second Adam? What does it mean to be adopted into God's family? What is the significance of baptism and the church?*

REINFORCE

In the overarching narrative of scripture, there are 5 keys that help us unlock its full meaning. These keys function as lenses through which we can experience scripture in multicolor. Reinforce these keys before moving onto part 2.

Trinity	*God is an eternal community of agape love.*
The Sanctuary	*God dwells "with" us in time and history.*
Design	*God's universe is built on other-centered parameters.*
Rebellion	*God is at war with the Satan and his selfish empire.*
Redemption	*God saves us through the gift of Jesus's sacrifice.*

PART 2:
1. THE WAR

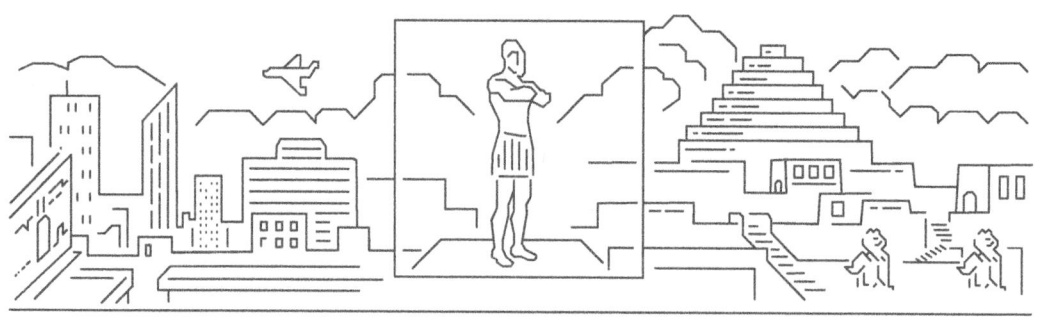

The story of scripture is liberating. And because liberation is at its heart, it's message cannot be fully understood or embodied, unless we accept that we need to be set free. And if we accept that we need to be set free, then we also accept that we are under an oppressive power that we cannot escape. Jesus taught this when he said that we are all slaves to sin. But he also said that his mission on Earth was to "set the captives free." And by "captives," he didn't simply mean people in physical restraints, but all of us. For Jesus, humanity is bound to a draconian spiritual system that has enslaved us for centuries.

This system is the true source of our suffering and the true fuel of injustice in the world. All forms of inhumanity, all manifestations of oppression, all abuses of our freedom and virtue, all marginalization, toxic power-differentials, and cruelty. All bloodthirsty empires, stolen lands, social inequity, and institutional discrimination. All racism, bigotry, coercion, and control that we see and struggle against and pray against, all of it is but a mere symptom of a deeper problem, a spiritual and trans-dimensional struggle involving what the apostle Paul referred to as, "the world's rulers of the darkness of this age, and against the spiritual forces of wickedness in the heavenly places" (Ephesians 6:12).

Now, that might sound a bit dark and gloomy, but no need to worry. This isn't going to be some traumatizing expose obsessing over all the big bad wolves in the Bible. Here, in the second leg of our journey, we are going to explore the themes that touch all of us: suffering, injustice, oppression, and trauma. And the purpose of this won't be to wallow in the negative, but to celebrate the light, the goodness, and the promise of a new civilization restored to Creator's original design of love.

Understanding the War

But before we do all that, we first need to see a clearer picture of this behind-the-scenes spirit war and how it affects all of us. According to scripture, the struggle began in a spiritual dimension, often referred to as "heaven," and then spread to the earth where it continues to this day. The apostle John and the prophets Isaiah and Ezekiel describe it as a cosmo-political (rather than a physical) war (Revelation 12:4, Isaiah 14:13, Ezekiel 28:17). Meaning, this war isn't about strength, power, or territory. It's a war over hearts, minds, and ideas.

Our first glimpse of this cosmic struggle is back in the Garden of Eden, where our story as a species began.

Read and discuss Genesis 3:1.

_____

_____

_____

We know that this serpent was a medium that the Satan used to trick Eve. But pay special attention to the "politics" behind his words. What is he attempting to accomplish? What story is he telling? Even though he asks a question, like many questions, it is really a statement in disguise. Behind the serpent's question is the assertion: "God is withholding something from you." The serpent attacks the very identity of God.

Read Genesis 3:4–5 and discuss what happens next.

_____

_____

_____

The serpent now accuses God of being a liar. He is no longer insinuating doubt—he is broadcasting it: "God cannot be trusted!" This is the same message he used to lead one-third of the angels in heaven to rebel against God (Revelation 12:3–9). And he continues to use it to induce separation and cosmic chaos. So, while there is a narrative of God's love in the Bible, we are also introduced to a counter-narrative that charges God with being self-centered, coercive, and unworthy of ruling the universe.

It was perhaps for this reason that the Satan said, "I will exalt my throne above the stars of God…" (Isaiah 14:13). In the midst of his rebellion, this meta-rival appears to promote the idea that he could govern better than God. To this day, the war between good and evil is a war of ideas and principles. Selfless love versus self-seeking empires. Creator (source of love) on the throne, or something else.

Read verses 6–8 of Genesis 3. What was the result of believing the serpent?

_____

_____

_____

With the entry of sin, mankind entered into a state of divine-human separation. We now hide from God. The very fabric of reality has been torn. God's harmonic creation has been infected with a foreign substance that gives birth to lies, selfishness, and relational separation. A new government arises to challenge Creator's way—one that rejects his love and goodness, questions his character, and attempts to usurp his place. And yet, God, in his unchanging nature, responds by doing something amazing.

Read verse 21 of Genesis 3. How does God respond to man's rejection?

_____

_____

Genesis 3:21 introduces us to a God unknown in all of religion. This Genesis 3:21 god doesn't condemn. Instead, he clothes Adam and Eve with the skin of a creature that represented his self-sacrifice. By clothing them, he promises that one day the fall will be reversed, shame will be erased, and oneness will be restored—not through humanity's efforts or sacrifices, but through Creator's own. Even in the madness of chaos and rebellion, God's love breaks through with relational integrity and communal passion. Despite the lies, the truth cannot be hidden. God loves us, likes us, and wants to be with us forever—even if it costs him everything. Paul captured the essence of this when he wrote,

"For one will hardly die for a righteous man. Yet perhaps for a good person someone would even dare to die. But God commends his own love toward us, in that while we were yet sinners, Christ died for us" (Romans 5:7–8).

How Does God Win this War?

After the US-led invasion of Iraq, things began to disintegrate rather quickly. The military presence, while initially celebrated, quickly wore out its welcome. As the years went by and the war dragged on, strategists realized that they could never win by sheer force. Even though the allied forces had more money, technology, and better weapons, it wasn't enough. What they finally realized was that this war was primarily about ideas, and the only way to win was to change the ideas of the people. Such a task could not be accomplished by force. Therefore, even though the invading armies had all the power, they had to limit their use of power, make themselves vulnerable, and begin to build relationships with the locals. In doing so, they would win the hearts and minds of the people, which would eventually result in victory.

This illustration helps us understand how God fights his enemy, the meta-rival of scripture. It's not a war about who is more powerful. Clearly, Creator can squash a created being without breaking a sweat. But this is a war about ideas. The Satan's lies about God are what led mankind to rebel against God. Those lies began in heaven and continue to spread across the earth today. And so long as we believe these lies about God, we will be held captive by them.

So, how can God fight back? There is only one way. God must reveal himself with the aim of changing how we see and feel about him. Only by the persuasion of love would our love for him be awakened. God would have to lay his power aside and make himself vulnerable, in order to win our hearts by love, not force. This plan of redemption was formulated by God before the world even began. As a result, God's character of self-sacrificing love is revealed immediately following Adam and Eve's rebellion. No sooner had mankind believed the lies about God than God responded by revealing the truth about himself. In Genesis 3:21, as skin covered the shame of our first parents, God prefigured his own sacrifice through which all of us would be restored. Genesis 3:21 pointed forward to the death of his own son and provided Adam and Eve with the hope of redemption.

Enter Israel...

But God didn't stop with Adam and Eve. Instead, he continued to reveal himself to their descendants until he eventually chose the nation of Israel to reveal his love to the entire world. It was Israel's unique birthright to communicate his love to the nations around them. Because of this special calling, the prophet Ezekiel could write, "[T]en men will take hold... of the skirt of him who is a Jew, saying, "We will go with you, for we have heard that God is with you'" (Zechariah 8:23). And Jesus could say, "salvation is from the Jews" (John 4:22).

All through the Old Testament, it was Israel's mission to reveal the God of Genesis 3:21 to a world that had bought into the lies. It was also through the lineage of Israel that Jesus would come to "crush the serpents head."

Not surprisingly, 1 Chronicles 21:1 tells us "Satan stood up against Israel..." Eventually, a combination of his efforts and Israel's own departure from God resulted in social collapse. The nation lost its way, the leaders became corrupt, and social injustice became the norm of the land. In a moment of agony, Jesus wept over this nation when he said, "Jerusalem, Jerusalem, who kills the prophets and stones those who are sent to her! How often I wanted to gather your children together, the way a hen gathers her chicks under her wings, and you were unwilling" (Matthew 23:37).

The rebellion went so far that eventually the religious leaders conspired with the Roman state to put Jesus to death. But God was not caught by surprise. He had a plan all along.

Read and discuss Galatians 3:29

_____
_____

The church—Christ's new humanity—is the continuation of true Israel. Jesus has given us the mission of revealing who God is and what he is like to a world that has been conned by the serpent's lies. But just as Lucifer rose up against Israel, the New Testament warns us that he would also rise up against the church.

Read the following verses to see how: 2 Corinthians 4:3–4, 11:3; 1 Timothy 4:1–5; and Acts 8:1–3. What picture do they paint about the future of the church and its story?

_____
_____

The New Testament's vision of the church's future isn't optimistic. According to the apostles, a falling away was coming—one in which the church itself would morph from an alternative community of love, to yet another system of oppression fueled by lies about God. With the spirit war raging at maximum force, the Satan made his next move. His greatest attack against God was soon to come. His greatest weapon of warfare and anti-Creator propaganda was soon to emerge. And you and I are smack in the middle of it.

As we begin our new leg of this journey, it is this tension that we are going to tackle the most. So if you have ever wondered, why has the church caused so much harm? Why is it so judgmental? So cruel? Why is its history filled with so much violence? Then hang in there. Things are about to get wild.

REFLECT

As beautiful as the gospel is, there is a darker side to the story. The Satan hates God, God's people, and most of all—the gospel. Consequently, he seeks to confuse, distort, and conceal the good news of God's love for humanity. His power is in the lies he tells—lies about God. This is why Paul said, "all who desire to live godly in Christ Jesus will suffer persecution" (2 Timothy 3:12). Because the church is the means by which God reveals his true identity to the world, this meta-rival has waged a war against it just as he did with the people of Israel in the Old Testament. In the coming chapters, we will dig deeper into the church-empire and explore the war between the narrative and the counter-narrative, its relation to the church, and how the truth about who God is and what he is like remains the only hope for the redemption of humanity.

CONNECT

Review _____
_____

Open _____
_____

Ask _____
_____

Decide _____
_____

ENGAGE

Scan the QR code to watch this chapter's accompanying Reflection video.

SCAN ME: THE WAR

2. THE EMPIRES

In the previous chapter, we looked deeper at the cosmo-political war the Bible describes. Led by a spirit being known as "the Satan" (meaning "the accuser") we saw that this war is fundamentally a struggle over ideas. The Satan's aim is to spread as many God-lies as possible in order to keep our world under his matrix of control. Ultimately, this rebellion is the root cause of all the injustice and chaos our planet has experienced for thousands of years.

Understanding the struggle between good and evil (God's goodness and the Satan's lies) really takes off in the apocalyptic books of Daniel and Revelation. In these books, written by men suffering the weight of systemic oppression and violence, the veil that hides the spiritual war at play around us is pulled back and we are given a glimpse into things that are otherwise hidden from our sight. Our journey, therefore, moves into a book written by a sage named Daniel.

Look up Daniel 2 and read verses 1–12. Summarize the story so far:

_____

_____

_____

Before moving on, pay close attention to verse 11. The wisemen reply to the king, "the thing which the king demands is difficult, and there is no one else who could declare it to the king except gods, *whose dwelling place is not with mortal flesh.*"(NIV)

In other words, while the gods of Babylon were supposedly powerful beings, they could not be consulted. The issue Nebuchadnezzar was dealing with was too personal, too intimate, and too difficult for the gods. This statement sets the contrast for what happens next. The king was soon to encounter a different kind of God. A God who—as we saw in Part 1—had the Israelites make him a sanctuary so that he could "dwell among them." This God is personal, intimate, and longs to dwell with us. Despite being the eternal other—our Creator who exists independent of us—he journeys closely and dwells with us as a friend.

So, back to the story. When the magicians were unable to do what the king asked, Nebuchadnezzar ordered that they all be killed (Daniel 2:12). However, Daniel intervened and prayed for God to reveal the dream to him. The sanctuary-God heard him and answered his prayer. What follows is the beginning of one of scriptures most shocking behind-the-scenes glimpses into the war between good and evil. Read verses 27–36 and fill in the spaces on the left below. Then, turn to verses 36–43 for the interpretation.

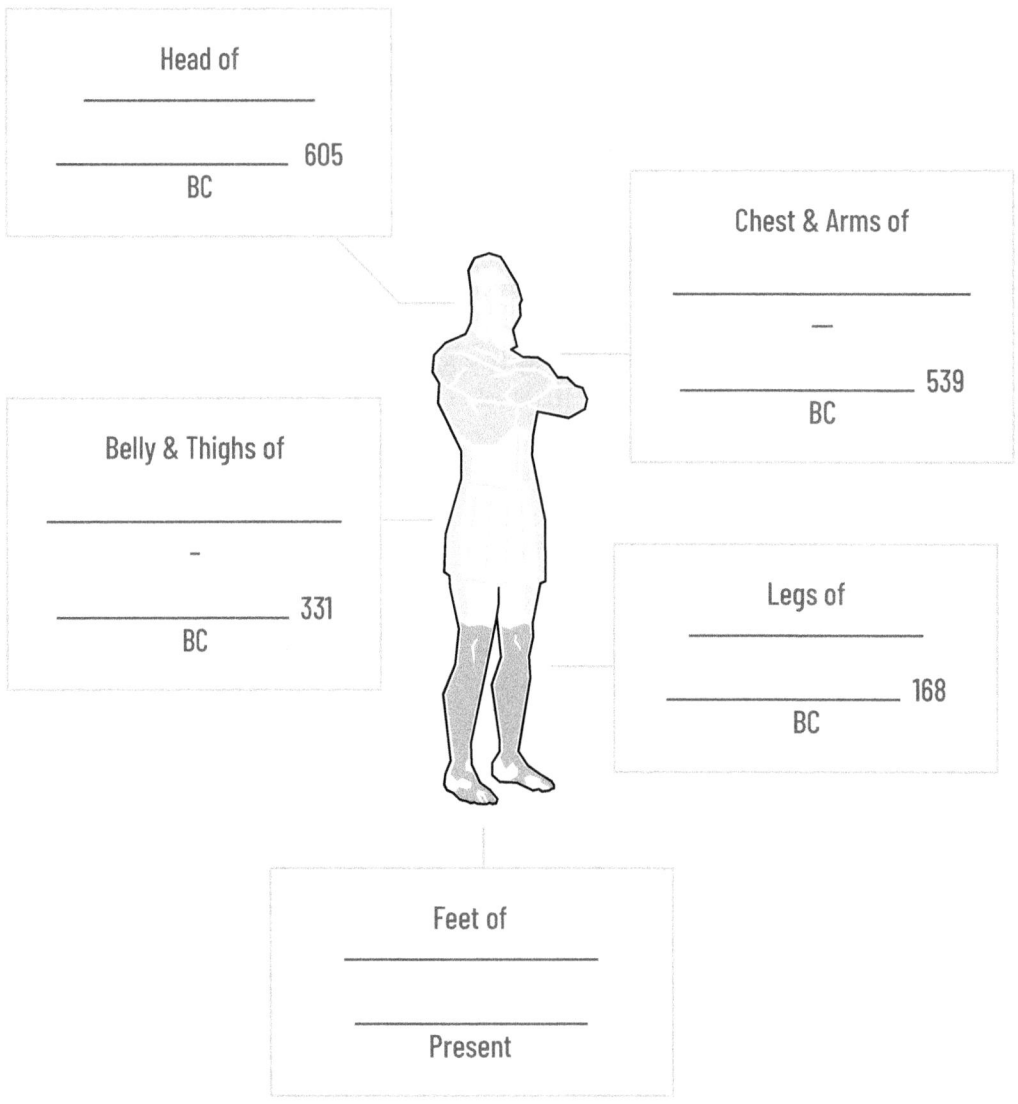

Apologies to everyone who is allergic to history and dates. Please, hang in there. It's worth it! Daniel is clear that the head of gold is Babylon. Historically, Daniel is speaking with Nebuchadnezzar around the year 605BC, just after the Babylonians conquered Jerusalem. Following historical records, the next kingdom to rise to power were the Medes and Persians whose reign began in 539BC. Then came the Greeks in 331BC and the Romans in 168BC. And of course, history confirms that Rome was never conquered. Instead it splintered due to repeated invasions, political instability, and internal corruption.

Now check this: Nebuchadnezzar had his dream around the year 605BC and through it Daniel sees events that were to take place from a few years ahead to centuries in the future. He saw the rise of Media-Persia 66 years before it happened, the rise of Greece 274 years before, and the rise of Rome 437 years ahead of time. But perhaps the most remarkable part is how Daniel saw the division of the Roman Empire 1081 years before it took place.

It's one thing for a supposed prophet to predict that a few nations would come and go. After all, any student of kingdoms would be able to guess that eventually Babylon would be conquered by another nation and then another would arise after that. But Daniel goes beyond this. Not only does he see the next four kingdoms that would follow Babylon, he also sees the destiny of the last kingdom as one that, rather than being conquered, would be divided forever like "iron and clay." History harmonizes with the dream. Nebuchadnezzar's vision has been fulfilled right down to the division in Rome that continues into our modern age.

However, this vision is not really about dates and kings—it's about much more. The dream opens to view the failure of human society. Each of these systems, built upon exploitation and oppression, would rise to the top by conquering, displacing, and profiting from one another. And at the height of their power, they would always implode. By rejecting Creator, (the source of agape love) these empires, following in the steps of the meta-rival, became gods unto themselves: Caught in this self-perpetuating loop, the agape life force of God was replaced by the impulse of self.

This impulse is the force that has governed every earthly dynasty throughout history. It has been the prime motivator of kings, councils, and senators. Its self-centered DNA has been deeply embedded in the very fabric of the political structure of one regime after another. And the result has always been the same. Temporary success built on injustice and coercion, only for a new kingdom to arise and take over.

The pages of history are replete with the blood of the innocent, the cries of widows, the groans of the orphans, the tears of slaves, and the despair of the dispossessed. Over and over, nation after nation has risen to the top of economic wealth, political supremacy, and resource control by exploiting the weak and the voiceless. And the consistent patterns of these governments have been the same throughout history: *they never last*.

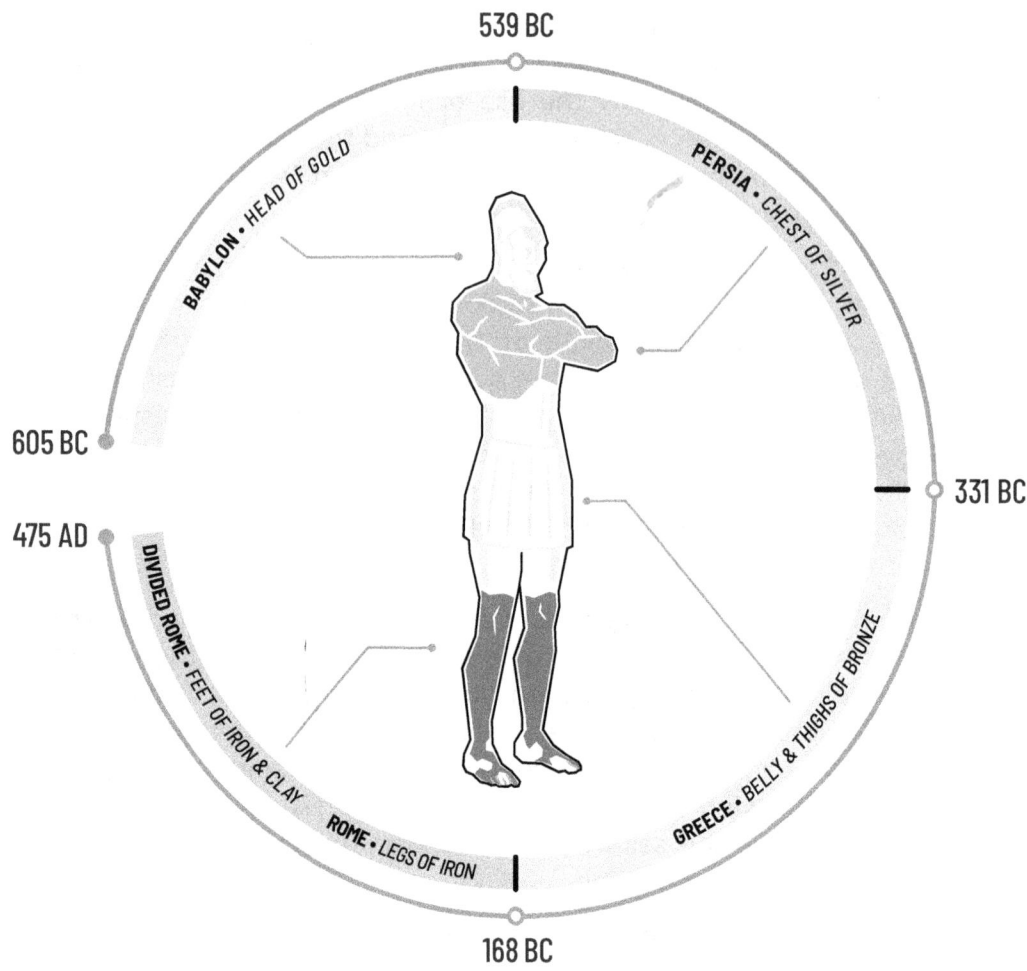

Daniel had just opened the veil to Nebuchadnezzar. His kingdom would be just like the others (Daniel 2:5). Proud as he may be of his accomplishments, he had arrived at his stature only by climbing upon the mountain of cadavers his armies littered across the land. And very soon, another would come to do the same to him. Then another, and another. Finally, the kingdom of Rome, mightier than the rest, would never be replaced by another kingdom but it would be divided, never to unite again. The division would continue until, at last, it would be evident that a kingdom built upon the principles of self could never stand. And in response, God would do something amazing.

Read and comment on verses 34–35 and 44–45 of Daniel 2. How does the vision end and what does it mean for you?

_____
_____
_____

The vision ends with a promise that human empire will one day be annihilated and replaced by a new kingdom that will never end. This kingdom is the kingdom of love, compassion, and relational integrity that Jesus came to reveal. It is a kingdom in which the strangling power of systemic and institutional injustice have no place, the exploiter and oppressor cannot enter in, and the social structures, conventions, and postures that oppress and harass will be forever erased. This new kingdom, constructed entirely on the foundation of God's heart of love, self-sacrifice, and justice, will replace all human empires.

And the best part is, it will never end.

HEALING TEACHING

Throughout history, empires have always risen to power through exploitation and abuses of power. Sadly, many religious ideologies picture God as no different to the emperors and kings whose lust for power drove them to the apex of luxury and control. However, scriptures portrait of God is entirely different. He is not a power-hungry cosmic dictator. To the contrary, he is an eternal community who longs for a cosmos restored to the rhythms of other-centred love.

REFLECT

Daniel, the "seer," saw the rise and fall of the four major world empires and it all happened just as he foresaw. Over 1000 years before it took place, he also saw the division of Rome and its failed attempts to reunite. We are living in that time now. But what the visions most clearly reveal is a cosmic war between two kingdoms. One kingdom is the kingdom of men ruled by selfishness, the other is the Kingdom of God ruled by love. This final kingdom is the only one yet to be seen and it is a kingdom that, according to Daniel, "will never end." Unlike the others, this kingdom will last because it will be based on the law of love rather than the law of self.

CONNECT

Review _____
_____

Open _____
_____

Ask _____
_____

Decide _____
_____

ENGAGE

Scan the QR code to watch this chapter's accompanying Reflection video.

SCAN ME: THE EMPIRES

3. THE BEAST

The Bible introduces us to a God of love and closeness. He created us for his love and, through the sanctuary, he communicates his desire to "dwell with us." Sin then enters the story, introducing a spiritual vacuum—a kind of tear in the fabric of reality that caused divine-human separation. But no sooner was sin here than Creator initiated a process of reversal and restoration. That process involved an unknown community of shepherds and slaves who eventually became the nation of Israel. And through this people, messiah Jesus would come and liberate all people. The gathering of "all people" into the new family of God is what the Bible calls church. This underground community would enact the kingdom of love in a world dominated by selfish empires. But the scriptures warn, the church would eventually lose its way.

Look up Daniel 7 and read verses 1–6, then discuss the images below:

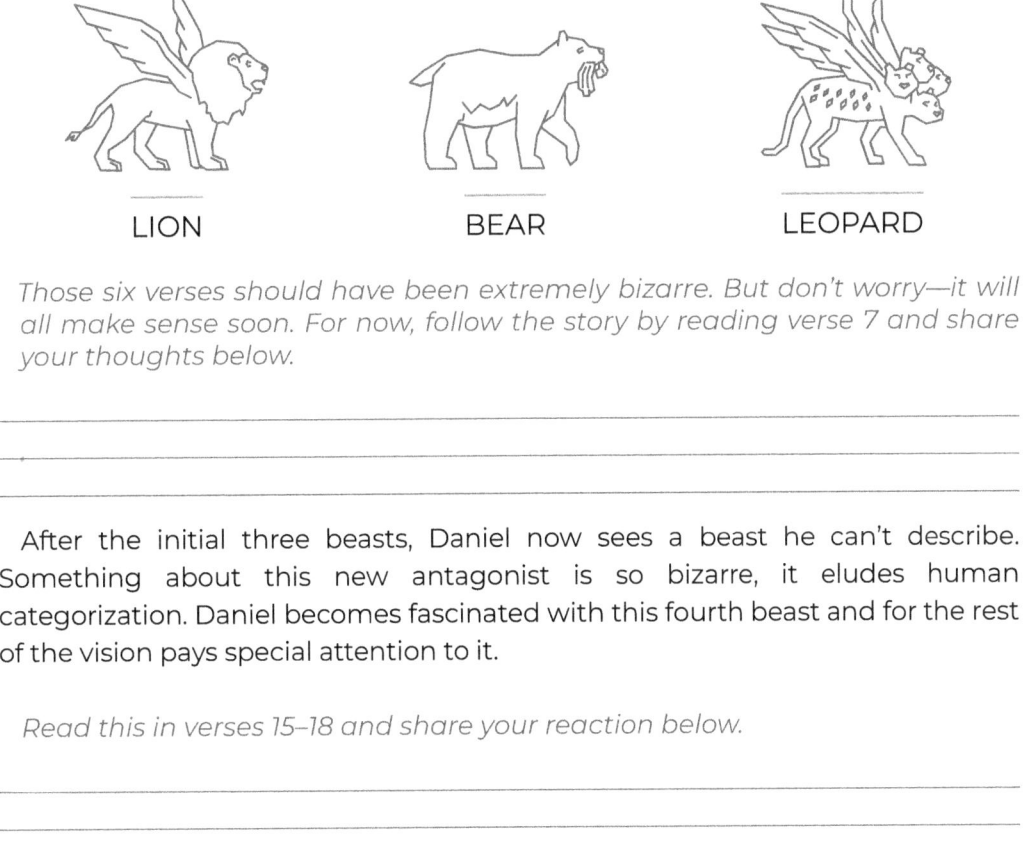

LION   BEAR   LEOPARD

Those six verses should have been extremely bizarre. But don't worry—it will all make sense soon. For now, follow the story by reading verse 7 and share your thoughts below.

_____
_____
_____

After the initial three beasts, Daniel now sees a beast he can't describe. Something about this new antagonist is so bizarre, it eludes human categorization. Daniel becomes fascinated with this fourth beast and for the rest of the vision pays special attention to it.

Read this in verses 15–18 and share your reaction below.

_____
_____
_____

Notice that Daniel 7 and Daniel 2 are really the same vision. The winged lion is Babylon, the head of gold. Archaeologists have shown that the kingdom of Babylon was often depicted as a lion with wings, making this a fitting symbol. At the time of writing, Babylon had already been conquered by the Medo-Persian Empire which is represented by the lopsided bear with three ribs in its mouth. The bear was raised up on one of its sides just as the Medes were more powerful than the Persians. In addition, the bear had three ribs in its mouth, likely representing three major nations they had devoured: Lydia, Babylon and Egypt.

Greece, still 208 years in the future, is represented by the flying leopard—a symbol of its speed. When Alexander the Great conquered the Mediterranean world, he was swift and unstoppable. The four heads of the leopard likely predicted Alexander's four generals (Cassander, Lysimachus, Seleucus and Ptolemy) who split Greece among themselves after Alexander's death.

However, interesting (or not) as all this might be, Daniel bypasses these first three beasts rather quickly. He is awestruck with the fourth, and wants to understand what it represents.

As we follow the historical timeline, we discover that the fourth beast is none other than the kingdom of Rome. Although it is still in the future (from Daniel's vantage point) Rome is the beast with iron teeth that crushes and devours everything—a fitting description of the most powerful empire that has ever ruled the earth. The ten horns, as we will soon see, represent its fall 1015 years before it actually took place.

As noted above, this vision is the same as Daniel 2, only with more detail. And in this vision, Daniel takes a special interest in the fourth kingdom. Read verses 19–25 then write down the descriptions below:

BEAST

Beast
_____
_____
_____
_____

The Other Horn
_____
_____
_____
_____

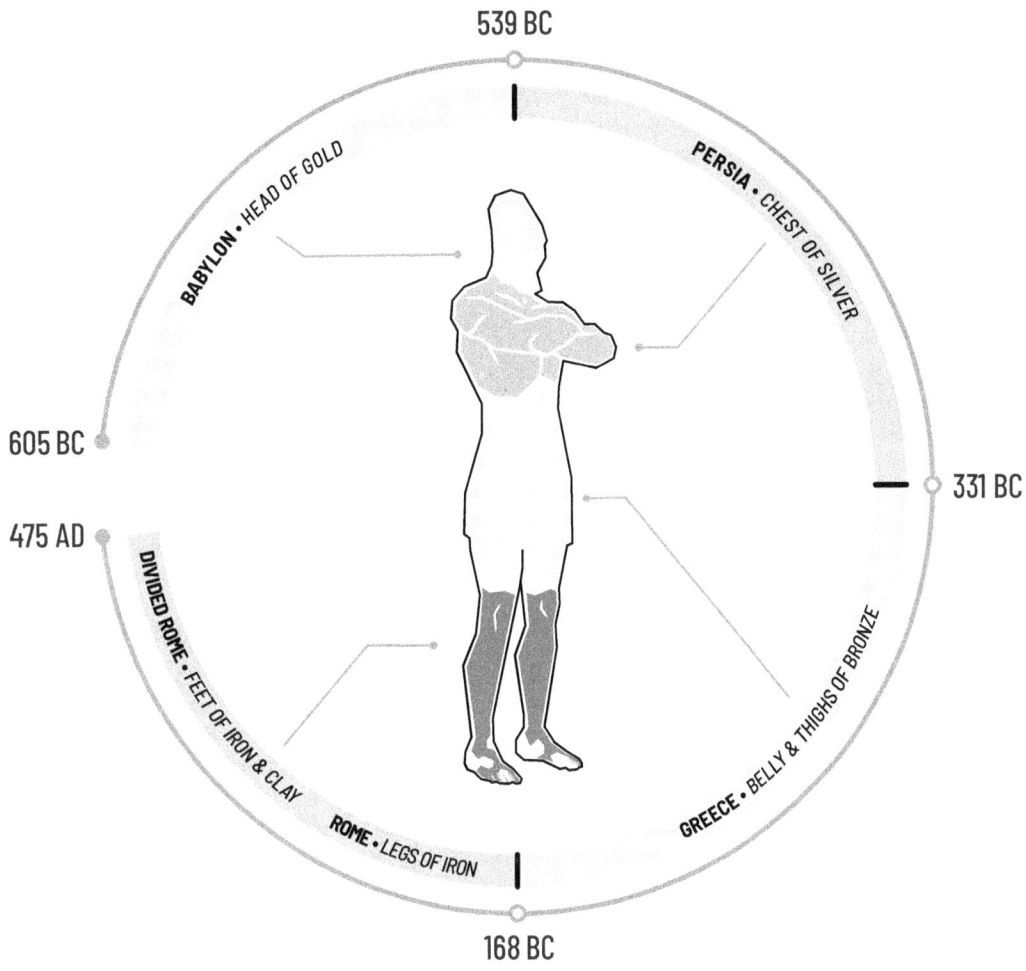

Don't get so caught up in the imagery that you miss the narrative. This final beast seems to be a main antagonist against God and represents the iron nation of Rome. The ten horns foretold how the once-unified nation would collapse and splinter. Now, the history of Rome's fall is long, complex and messy—too much for us to explore in detail.

In fact, the details of this entire vision are way too intense to cover in this chapter. But no need to worry! If you don't mind history, dates, and cracking secret codes, the QR code on the next page contains a PDF download that explains this entire vision in detail.

Scan here to download chapter supplement

SCAN ME: THE BEAST

In the remainder of this chapter, we are going to keep things simple (no more dates) and unpack what this bizarre dream, written thousands of years ago, means for us in the here and now. And the whole thing comes together once we follow Daniel, as he sets his gaze on one of the vision's most bizarre characters: A horn called "other" who rises to the apex of power.

The "Other" Horn

The Russian novelist Fyodor Dostoevsky once said, "People speak sometimes about the 'bestial' cruelty of man, but that is terribly unjust and offensive to beasts, no animal could ever be so cruel as a man, so artfully, so artistically cruel."

Although we can't know for sure, Dostoevsky might have been reacting to the notion that human empire is a "beast"—an idea popularized by Italian philosopher Niccolo Machiavelli. For Dostoevsky, calling human empires "beasts" was an insult to beasts, because no beast ever engineered systems of enslavement, marginalization, or exploitation.

The Bible seems to agree. While it certainly calls empires "beasts," notice that none of the beasts actually exist. They are all mutant-like—a lion with wings, a lopsided bear, a leopard with four heads. But notice this as well, when the vision arrives at the final beast, it doesn't describe it using any creatures we are familiar with. Whatever Daniel saw, it was so cruel, that no terrestrial beast could adequately represent it—not even a mutated version.

This final empire, the kingdom of Rome, rose to the mountain top of power. And as we have already seen, all human empires get to the top by trampling on whatever is beneath. So, Daniel describes this kingdom as one that crushes, devours and then tramples on whatever is left. He describes it as terrifying and frightening—a beast with power unlike any other, with a legacy of victims in its wake. The final beast, however, has ten horns, and out of the ten, an "other" emerges to take the legacy of injustice to heights never before seen.

Daniel describes this new level of systemic injustice in verses 8, 20–21, and 25. Write your own summary of what this horn does below.

___

___

___

Notice that this horn seems to have a special focus. Far from being a mere political power pursuing terrestrial domination, this horn wars against God. It has eyes like a man (human empire), a mouth speaking boastfully (propaganda), and it attacks the holy people—that is the alternative "kingdom of love" community that Jesus launched in the New Testament. And the horn succeeds. Its systemic and institutional matrix of control and domination take it to the apex of elitism—far beyond the reach of human justice. It prospers in everything.

Who is the "Other" Horn?

Identifying this other horn is really simple. Just follow the vision in Daniel 7. According to the angel's description, the Roman empire would divide into 10 kings. Out of this division emerges the other horn. It destroys three of the ten kings and launches a religious war against God by spreading lies (boastful mouth) about God. It would oppress and silence anyone who opposed it, and reach such heights of religio-political control that it would be above human justice.

And the uncomfortable and hard-to-swallow truth is that there is only one power in all of history that emerged out of the fallen Roman Empire that fits this exact description: *The Christian church*.

Let that sink in. Read it again if you have to.

Scan the QR code above for the expanded version of this chapter if you need to.

Because that last paragraph, its wild. And if true—it changes everything.

How is Christianity the "Other" Horn?

By AD400 Christianity had become the official religion of the Roman Empire—a political, as well as a religious, power. It destroyed three kings that opposed it and became the dominant political power of Rome. It also warred against God by claiming to be his ally while appropriating his image to fit their pursuit of temporal power. It imprisoned, tortured, and killed those who protested its oppression and presented God as an arbitrary and punitive being. The crusades, the inquisition, the political subterfuge and spiritual abuse that dominates the church's history is predicted in Daniel's dream. Thousands of years before the church was even a thing, God revealed the depths to which it would sink.

Jesus had commissioned the church to tell his story, and, like Israel before it, the church became the main perpetrator of lies about God—not only in what it taught, but in its social impact. Read and discuss Zephaniah 3:1; Acts 7:51–53, 20:29–30; and 2 Corinthians 11:12–15. What light do these texts shed on Daniel's vision?

Read also Daniel 7:9–12, 26. What is it that happens to this other horn?

_____

_____

_____

While the church enjoyed over 1000 years of uncontested power, it was eventually overthrown by Napoleon Bonaparte during the French Revolution. Christianity's uncontested oppressive rule had come to an end.

Daniel reveals, with stunning clarity, the war between good and evil at play in the most unexpected of places: *the history of the church*.

But this is more than just history. It is personal. As we survey the legacy of Christianity as an empire, we see very little of the person of Jesus reflected in its trail of sadness. To this day, the blood of indigenous tribes and native children, spilled by the church, cries to us from the ground. The trauma of "holy wars," inquisitions, and decades of unjust, tyrannical governance seems to haunt us still. But it's even deeper than this. For the littered landscape left behind by Christendom reaches beyond these grand tales and into the hearts and homes of every-day people. Children who have been abused, women who have been oppressed, divorcees who have been humiliated, and LGBTQI+ teens who have been abandoned, often driven to lifelong mental suffering and even suicide.

And the trail is not past tense. It continues even to the modern age; as Christian nationalists reach desperately for political power, seemingly oblivious to the collateral suffering caused by the blending of church and state. And it will go on, until at last, the closing scenes of Daniel's vision are fulfilled.

In my vision at night I looked,
and there before me was one like a son of
man, coming with the clouds of heaven.
He approached the Ancient of Days
and was led into his presence. He was given
authority, glory and sovereign power;
all nations and peoples of every
language worshiped him.
His dominion is an everlasting dominion
that will not pass away, and his kingdom
is one that will never be destroyed...
It will be an everlasting kingdom.

DANIEL 7:13–14, 27 (NIV)

REFLECT

A few decades after the last of the apostles died, the church took a dive. The gospel was distorted into a religious institution, grace was erased, and the story of God replaced by a counter-narrative that misrepresented his character. The serpent's lies in Eden had now infiltrated the church and became its narrative. And the question that this part of the story forces us to think about is this: How long? How long would God allow injustice to move so freely? How long would the church get away with its lies? How long until he finally fought back? How long would it be until the lies were exposed, the gospel restored, and the truth about his character of love reintroduced to the world?

CONNECT

Review _____

Open _____

Ask _____

Decide _____

ENGAGE

Scan the QR code to watch this chapter's accompanying Reflection video.

SCAN ME: THE BEAST

4. THE OTHER

In the last chapter, we discovered that the war between good and evil has been raging in the background for centuries. It began in heaven as a war over the character of God and now it continues here on the earth. The nation of Israel, with its special calling to tell the world about God's love, turned its back on God, was conquered by the Babylonians, and remained under the oppression of Greece, Medo-Persia and Rome. After Jesus's death, and during the time Rome was the world power, the church was commissioned to continue telling the true story of God. But not long after the death of the apostles, the church too began to fall away. After the fall of Rome, it emerged as a religious and political power and oppressed the people under its rule for over 1000 years.

So far, we have managed to make sense of Daniel's description of the church's war against God in this way:

Other Horn	*Church gains political power*
Destroys 3/10 Horns	*Church terminated opposition*
Blasphemous	*Church engineered a counter-narrative*
Horn Grows	*Church becomes an empire*
Wears Out Saints	*Institutional and systemic oppression*
Against God	*Anti-Christ systems and propaganda*
Rules 1260 Years	*Was untouchable and unstoppable*

However, while the other horn's oppressive rule ended, the lies it told about God did not end with it. Instead, they continued to spread, almost uncontested, and do so to this day. As a result, there exist two competing narratives in the modern age. During his earthly journey, Jesus worked to reveal the Father to us, providing the church with a narrative built on the truth about God. For over 1000 years, the meta-rival worked, via the church, to bury the truth Jesus revealed and fill the world with a counter-narrative, built on lies about God. These two opposing narratives remain at war all around us.

How do we make sense of this war, its implication for us, and its relevance for our world? First we need to go back to the vision. Read Daniel 7:25.

What exactly does the phrase "think to change times and laws" mean? Turn also to Daniel 2:19–21 for a hint.

_____

_____

_____

Times

Recall that, in Daniel 2, Nebuchadnezzar had a dream that the magicians could not reveal to him. In his anger, he threatened to have all of the wise men of Babylon killed. Daniel prayed to God and God revealed the dream to him. As Daniel praises God, he attributes to him the power to "change times..." (verse 21), which he then equates with "setting kings up and taking them down."

In other words, God has veto power over the human chess board. He possesses ultimate authority over human history (times), and while he doesn't script the movements of history (determinism), he has the power to maneuver them toward a redemptive end.

The vision of Daniel 2 reveals the rise and fall of major empires, all of which were used by the Satan in his war against God. Yet it was God who "set" the time for those kingdoms to rise and fall, and it was he who raised up their kings and removed them. Even in the war between good and evil, God is no victim. He allows free beings to rebel, but he never abdicates his authority. While men have free will to engineer systems of oppression, God still draws a line in the sand and, ultimately, they will all come to a complete end.

The Christian church, drunk with political power, took it upon itself to claim what only belonged to God—the ability to "change times." It persecuted, manipulated, and oppressed all, in an attempt to establish a kingdom on Earth of its own liking. It rose to the pinnacle of power—gaining control even over the royal rulers of nations—and was responsible for war, bloodshed, and injustice. In all of this, the Satan was attempting to claim authority over human history or "times." As a result of the religious oppression, many came to see God as depicted by the fallen church. Rather than a God of love and justice, he came to be seen as an oppressive tyrant.

Law

The text also says that the horn would seek to change the law.

Look up Matthew 22:38–39, Romans 13:10, and Galatians 5:14. What do these texts reveal about God's law?

_____
_____
_____

The law in scripture is not something that is declared and enforced arbitrarily. Rather, the law reflects the very agape-love character of Creator and reveals the way in which he designed reality to work. In other words, the law is not something you keep because "God told you so." Rather, it is the very fabric of reality and it is based on God's character of love.

The Sabbath is a perfect example. While it is a commandment, it is simultaneously much more. The Sabbath celebrates our value as human beings; our connection to the earth and its creatures; the equality of all, including migrants and refugees; and its rhythms stand in protest to the values of consumerism and commodification. You are not a product, not merchandise, not an object. The fabric of reality, the design of God's universe says otherwise. You are a deeply consequential and unique being whose very form and consciousness is patterned after divinity itself.

But along comes the other horn, thinking to change laws. As the church began to fall away, the view of the law changed from "design" to "arbitrary." As a result, the law of love came to be regarded as an imposed set of rules, rather than a loving design for human flourishing. Consequently, God came to be viewed as more of a dictator/emperor than a creative designer. And because the church claimed to be the direct representative of this tyrannical God, it was able to exploit unprecedented levels of political power.

But it doesn't stop there. When you have a law of design based on God's character of love, then it logically follows that such a law cannot be changed unless God himself changes. But when you have an imposed set of rules with no design to them, rooted in a controlling deity, then it logically follows that such a law can be arbitrarily altered given the right amount of power. The church, as a mark of its authority, did just this by altering the Sabbath commandment. As a result, the very command that celebrates God's creative beauty was replaced by a command that honors the power of the church-empire. Thus, in 1400, an Italian juror named Petrus de Ancharano could say,

> "The pope can modify divine law, since his power is not of man, but of God, and he acts in the place of God upon earth, with the fullest power of binding and loosing his sheep."[1]

Likewise Gaspare de Fosso, one of the churches archbishops, could declare,

> "The Sabbath, the most glorious day in the law, has been changed into the Lord's Day."—Sunday—"These and other similar matters have not ceased by virtue of Christ's teaching, but they have been changed by the authority of the church."[2]

Notice the focus on "power" and "authority." The church-empire was not simply trying to climb the ladder of human power. It was, in its fullest sense, the greatest weapon the Satan had ever engineered in his war against God. Rather than an anti-God system, insulting Creator, the church-empire claimed allegiance to him while simultaneously giving the world an image of his heart that was repulsive. With the lies and trauma-inducing system in full effect, fewer and fewer people would want to trust in God. The plan worked, and to this day, it continues to dominate the way most people think about God.

"Think"

However, there is a key word in Daniel's vision that we cannot miss: *think*. This word means to "intend or hope." In other words, the enemy of Creator would think (or hope) to defeat God through its lies, but it would not succeed. Think or hope as it might, healing and truth would win the day. Love is just too powerful, too mesmerizing, and too resilient. And in time, as the clock of history moved forward, love would pierce through the darkness and the spell of lies would break.

Read Malachi 3:6, Matthew 5:18, and Luke 16:17. How do these verses relate to the law of God? How do they help us understand his character and the war between good and evil?

_____
_____
_____

According to scripture, the law of God is not an arbitrary set of rules that he imposes on humanity. To the contrary, his law is a natural extension of his love. Far from a legal code, it is a natural in-built design parameter intended to nurture social, interpersonal, and divine-human relationship. By convincing the world that the law of God was an arbitrary set of demands enforced by threat of eternal punishment, the church-empire altered societies view of God's heart on a global scale. People became afraid of God, and, like Adam and Eve in the garden, they bought into the lies of the serpent. Today, many of us spend our lives hiding from God because we have been convinced that he is cruel and abusive. But nothing could be further from the truth.

Herein lies the beauty of Daniel's vision: Despite the corruption of the church, the lies spread by the accuser, and the suffering perpetuated by the very people who claimed allegiance to God—there will come a time where God's love will flood the earth like never before. Daniel 7 shows us that, despite the church-empire's propaganda campaign, love finds a way to restore justice and bring about true liberation.

_____

1. Petrus de Ancharano, quoted in Lucius Ferraris, "Papa," article 2 in *Prompta Bibliotheca*, vol. 6 (Venice: Gaspar Storti, 1772), 29. (emphasis added)

2. Gaspare de Fosso, quoted in Mansi, *Sacrorum Conciliorum*, 33:529, 530. (emphasis added)

REFLECT

The war between good and evil is far more intense and subtle than many of us realize. Through the influence of the church-empire, the law of God was changed from a law of design based on God's character of love, to an arbitrary law imposed by an authoritarian deity. Consequently, the church — also an authoritarian entity — showcased its power by arbitrarily changing the laws of God as a sign of its authority. This same oppressive nature was reflected in the church's political rule as well. But remember—this is not about the church. The true damage was on the character of God. The world now came to believe that God was a punitive, controlling, and distant deity. The sanctuary narrative was erased. The love of God was obscured. And the story Jesus came to tell was replaced by an alternate story that painted God in repulsive and frightening colors. And while the church's oppressive rule came to an end, the lies it perpetuated about God continue to be the primary source of most of humanity's perception of who God is and what he is like. This brings us back to the unanswered question: How long? How long until the suffering finally ends?

CONNECT

Review _____

_____

Open _____

_____

Ask _____

_____

Decide _____

_____

ENGAGE

Scan the QR code to watch this chapter's accompanying Reflection video.

SCAN ME: THE OTHER

5. THE RESET

The war between truth and lies about God is an ideological struggle far more dangerous than conventional warfare. In conventional war, it is your body that is at risk of harm. In ideological warfare, it is your inmost thoughts and beliefs—the very soul itself—that is at risk. So far, Daniel has shown us how this war of ideas is essentially the war that causes all wars. Lies about God have led to division and strife. Like a domino effect, this tension spills over into our daily lives impacting our self-direction, families, friendships and—on a larger scale—social relations. This, in turn, has led to a history of injustice in which empires and nations war against one another in a futile effort to get to the top. Even the church itself became an empire that perpetuated suffering and lies. We now dive into Daniel 8 where the prophet discloses how much longer this war, with all of its suffering and oppression, will last. Look up Daniel 8 and read verses 1–8.

RAM   GOAT

In this vision we see a Ram and a Goat. But there is more. Read verses 9–12. Who else is in this vision? And how is this character described (left column)? Read also verses 23–25 for a further description (right column).

The Other Horn

_____
_____
_____

The Insolent King

_____
_____
_____

Before we identify this character, read verses 20–22. Who are the Ram and the Goat?

_____
_____
_____

As the angel says, the Ram is Medo-Persia, with one horn larger than the other. The male goat is Greece, its prominent horn, also described as its first king, is Alexander the Great. The four horns to emerge after are likely his four generals who split Greece among themselves after Alexander's death. And, just as predicted, from this point forward the Greek nation never regained the power it had under Alexander.

The horn to emerge out of the four winds is the same as the other horn of Daniel 7: Rome and Christian Rome. Rome grew exceedingly great and conquered everything in its path, including the Beautiful Land of Israel. As it shifted from a political to a religio-political power, it became the Satan's main instrument of warfare against God. The heads of the church were known for their pomp, power, and divine status, which they used for political leverage. Worst of all, the church-empire corrupted the Jesus-way. In doing so, it "removed the regular sacrifice"—an Old Testament symbol pointing to the sacrifice of Jesus on the cross.

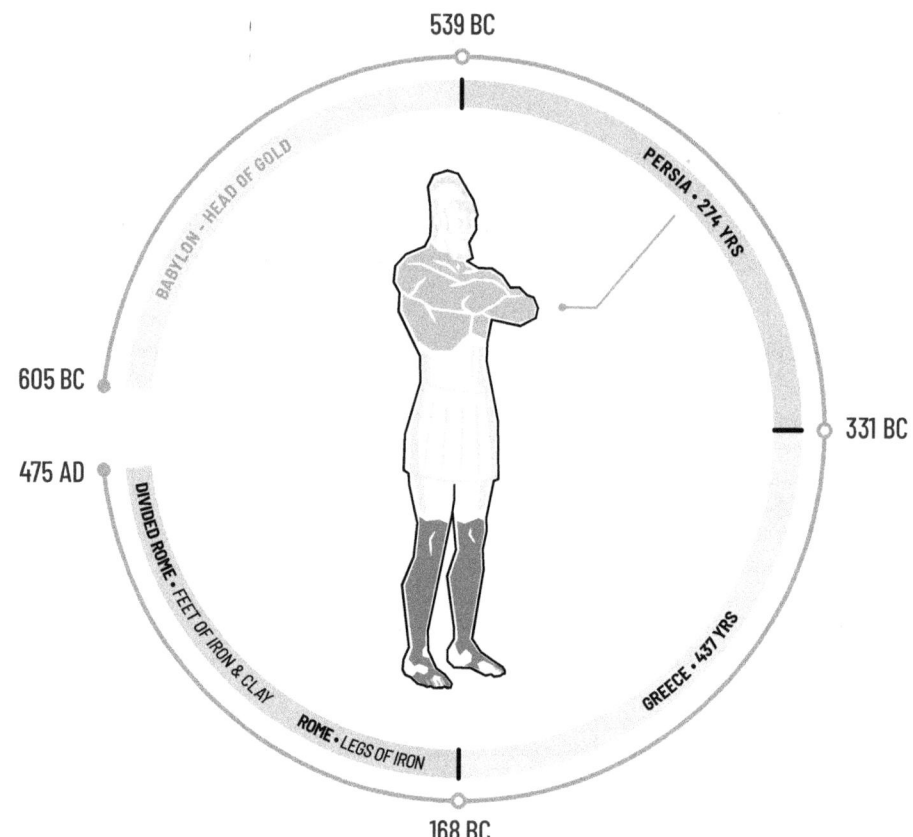

Daniel sees his prophetic vision, as recorded in Daniel 2 and 7, years before any of its events took place, but in Daniel 8 he gives even more detail. His description of Greece, 200 years ahead of time, is stunning. Bypassing much of Rome's secular phase, he focuses mostly on the church-empire waging its war against God, 1000 years before it unfolded, and the details are mind boggling. Daniel records how the church tyrannizes the innocent and wars against the prince of heaven by presenting a story of God founded on lies. In this way it "flung truth to the ground" and "caused deceit"—propaganda—"to prosper." And the worst part is, it stands unopposed! As Daniel sees the church waging a successful war against God, a being in the vision asks a heart-wrenching question.

Read Daniel 8:13–14. Comment on the question below.

_____
_____
_____

We can summarize the question like this: "How long?" But this is no ordinary question. To the contrary, it is a question saturated with grief—the kind you only ask when you find yourself immersed in profound suffering.

"How long?" opens to view the agony of heaven as an unknown being, overwhelmed by the trauma of cosmic warfare, asks: "How long will the arch-nemesis be allowed to raise empires and war against God? How long do we have to suffer under the burden of this war? How long until it finally ends? In fact, will this conflict ever end?"

The answer is yes, but the explanation given is bizarre. Notice the reply:

"IT WILL TAKE 2300 DAYS, THEN THE SANCTUARY WILL BE CLEANSED."
DANIEL 8:14

What do 2300 Days, a Sanctuary, and Cleansing Mean?

In order to comprehend the answer, we need to re-explore the narrative of the sanctuary with a bit more detail. Recall from Part 1 that in scripture we find a sanctuary in heaven that communicates God's desire to dwell with us in our time and space. From there, God had a sanctuary on the earth that communicated the same story through symbols, feasts, and metaphors. We don't know too much about heaven's sanctuary, but we do know that the Jewish one was a copy of the heavenly one (Exodus 25:9; Hebrews 8:5, 9:11). So, let's do a quick revision and see if we can decipher the meaning of Daniel 8:14.

LAMB   PRIEST   JUDGE

The sanctuary was divided into three rooms, which can be thought of as three scenes in a movie. The first scene was where the sacrifice of the lamb took place. The second scene was where the priest represented the sinner before God. The third scene was where judgment took place before the throne of God. Each of the scenes builds on the previous one and tells the story of God's plan of salvation for the entire human race. By giving this sanctuary to Abraham's descendants, God designed for them to be a "light to the nations" (Isaiah 49:5–6) and a "blessing to all people" (Genesis 12:1–3). Through it, God communicated his love and desire to dwell with his people despite the disruptive presence of sin.

1. The Lamb

The worshiper brings the lamb, representing Jesus, to the sanctuary. He confesses his sin over the lamb and the guilt is transferred. The innocent lamb dies in his place.

2. The Priest

The priest kills the lamb and takes the blood into the second room. In the second room, the priest presents the blood of the lamb on behalf of the worshiper, who has already gone home free.

3. The Judge

The priest enters the third room, where God's throne is, once a year. He presents a sacrifice on behalf of the community and "cleanses" the sanctuary and society of all record of sin (Leviticus 16).

The sanctuary tells the story of salvation as God administers it in our time and space. Scenes 1 and 2 were repeated, morning and evening, every day. Through them, the people were constantly reminded of their need for a savior and God's promise to provide salvation. We already explored these in pretty good detail in part 1, so in this chapter lets turn our attention over to the third scene.

The third scene took place once a year and was different to the first two. In this scene, God "cleanses" the entire community and the sanctuary. The Old Testament calls this third scene the "Day of Atonement," or "Judgment Day," and it involved the entire nation, not just individuals. The reason is simple, the Day of Atonement opens to view God's plan for social restoration by pointing to the time when God will reset the cosmos in order to eradicate sin and restore human civilization to perfect harmony with his heart. In short, the cleansing of the sanctuary is a metaphor pointing to a grand reset that ushers in true social reconstruction and cosmic healing.

Now this is pretty heavy stuff, especially for those of us living in a totally different culture to the ancient Israelite's, so lets try and simplify this. The sanctuary as a whole is all about Jesus and his redemptive plan for humanity. The first two scenes focus mostly on our individual restoration by centering on the individual bringing a sacrifice to the temple. The final scene, however, moves from the individual to the collective. It points to God's restorative reset of society by eradicating all injustice, oppression, and unjust structures. In short, the Sanctuary is the narrative of salvation from the empire of sin and God's pursuit of cosmic social justice, as it plays out in the entirety of the human story.

Back to Daniel

Let's go back to Daniel. The "other" horn has arisen. It twists the story of salvation and develops its own narrative. It turns people away from God and, through spiritual lies, amplifies divine-human separation and the fragmentation of society. The story of the sanctuary (love, withness, grace) is trampled on, and the "daily sacrifice" (Jesus's death that restores oneness) is "cast to the ground"—forgotten and tossed aside. Because the entire redemptive plan hinges on Jesus's sacrifice, the horn's suppression campaign appears to have succeeded in halting the process toward this cosmic/social renewal. Overwhelmed by it all, a being in the vision then asks, "how long?..." And an angel replies, "it will take 2300 days, then the sanctuary will be cleansed."

Now that we have explored the narrative of the sanctuary, we can decipher what the angel means. The 2300 days represent the time that would transpire before this event happened. When the years ended, the sanctuary would be cleansed—a reference to the time when the final judgment over sin and the reconstruction of humanity's global village would begin. And in this final judgment, three central events are at play:

 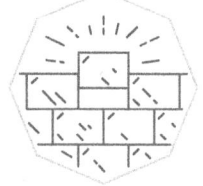 

Individual Restoration   **Social Reconstruction**   **Civilization Re-birthed**

1. Individual Restoration:

Through the sanctuary, every person is invited into restored oneness with God. By absorbing our separation and overcoming it, Jesus offers himself as the portal to a restored/transformational relationship (non-separation) with God.

2. Social Reconstruction:

When the priest removed the sin from the sanctuary in the Old Testament, he performed an act that symbolized the complete removal of the way of self, not merely from individuals, but from the community (Lev. 16). This points us toward God's reversal and healing—not just of individual human hearts, but of social, systemic, and institutional injustices. In short, God doesn't merely restore people, he rebirths society. In doing so, the judgment demonstrates that God isn't merely bringing independent beings into heaven, he is redeeming human civilization by birthing—in Jesus—a new humanity that moves to the rhythms of agape love.

3. New Civilization:

The end result of this process is the grand reset—a divine rebirthing of human civilization from the way of self to the rhythms of other-centered, agape love. It is a new society, populated by a civilization remade in the image of Jesus. This new civilization is tied to the teaching of the Second Adam and Humanity 2.0 that we explored in part 1. It is the ultimate culmination of God's redemptive plan.

REFLECT

God has appointed a day for judgment to begin. When the judgment is over, it will mark the end of the war between good and evil. The oppressive rule of kings and nations, along with the spiritual lies of the church-empire and every other system that has aligned itself with the enemy of love, will come to an end. A new civilization will then flourish, moving to the rhythms of God's love and constructing a global village in which equity, compassion, and servanthood (the way of Jesus) are the cornerstones.

CONNECT

Review ___

Open ___

Ask ___

Decide ___

ENGAGE

Scan the QR code to watch this chapter's accompanying Reflection video.

SCAN ME: THE RESET

6. THE ONE

In our previous studies on Daniel, we explored the battle between two kingdoms—a battle which culminates with the church-empire as the main antagonist against God. The visions conclude with the cleansing of the sanctuary at the end of a time period. This cleansing represents Creators pursuit of cosmic justice, through which the universe is restored. While the esoteric nature of the dream is bizarre, the message is simple: *Injustice is to have its way for a time, but once the timeline closes, the divine court will sit and the cleansing of the universe begins.*

The vision should fill anyone who reads it with hope. However, the opposite happened. Rather than hope, the story says that Daniel "fainted, and was sick for some days...[He] wondered at the vision, but no one understood it." (Daniel 8:27).

Read Daniel 9:20–23. What happens next?
Read the explanation in verses 24–27.

_____

_____

In the verses you just read, the angel Gabriel shows up to give Daniel a further explanation of the vision of the cleansing. However, if you are a normal human being, his explanation may have left you horribly confused. The language the angel uses is dizzying. The metaphors, foreign. What does any of it mean?

In this chapter, we are not going to unpack all the details of this vision. To be perfectly honest, this vision is one of the most intricate and mind-blowing prophecies in all of scripture, but it involves a lot of dates, history, and even a few calculations. And the truth is, not everyone's brain is wired to enjoy sorting through all those layers of intricate complexity.

So, in this chapter, we are going to focus on the main theme of the vision and leave the finer, geekier, details out. However, if you are one of those rare souls who enjoys deciphering enigmatic timelines with precision, the QR code on the next page contains a PDF download that explains the Daniel 9 vision in detail.

Feel free to download it and explore it after you finish this chapter. If you would rather not, that's totally fine. The contents of this chapter alone will explore the main point of the visions and what they have to say to the social injustices, religious trauma, and lies about God that dominate our culture.

Scan here to download chapter supplement

SCAN ME: THE ONE

In order to appreciate the existential significance of Daniel's dizzying and bizarre vision, we need to focus on the central point the angel is communicating to him. That central point is in verse 25. Unfortunately, this also happens to be the part of the vision where things get wildly confusing. So lets break it down and simplify it. Here is the first half:

> *"He"*—the angel Gabriel—*"explained to me, 'Daniel, I have come here to give you insight and understanding. The moment you began praying, a command was given. And now I am here to tell you what it was, for you are very precious to God. Listen carefully so that you can understand the meaning of your vision.'" (NLT)*

So far so good. Gabriel has basically said to Daniel, "Remember that vision on the cleansing of the sanctuary that freaked you out and left you exhausted and sick? Yeah... I'm here to tell you more."

But why did Daniel freak out? And why did he need more explanation? Isn't the point of the vision obvious? It began with a spirit being protesting the endless cycles of injustice and suffering by asking, "How long?" And the answer given—while odd to us—should have been pretty clear for Daniel. The cleansing of the sanctuary is an ancient Hebraic metaphor of God's complete restoration of the universe and the eradication of sin from the human heart and society as a whole. Didn't Daniel see that the whole vision was about the promise of divine, social justice; God healing human civilization; and a return to the rhythms of relational oneness God originally designed?

If so, then why did he need more explanation? And why did he freak out so much that he experienced not just emotional distress, but trauma-like biological events in his body (exhaustion, sickness)?

If the vision is as simple and straightforward as we explored in the previous chapter, then Daniel's response makes no sense. But perhaps the issue is: its not so straight forward. Something more is needed for it all to come together.

Let's take a look at what the vision says next:

A period of seventy sets of seven has been decreed for your people and your holy city to finish their rebellion, to put an end to their sin, to atone for their guilt, to bring in everlasting righteousness, to confirm the prophetic vision, and to anoint the Most Holy Place. (NLT)

Here is where things get super odd. And if you felt your eyes crossing over as you read this text, you are in good company. Its awfully confusing stuff, and a bit boring too. But it also helps us understand why Daniel was freaking out.

"Your People and Your Holy City"

Notice that in the text, the angel focuses entirely on the people of Israel—Daniel's people. He begins by saying, "a period of time has been set apart for *your people* and *your holy city."*

To do what? To, "finish their rebellion."

Why is Daniel freaking out? Because he knows that the vision is all about divine social justice. He knows God is going to restore all things. He knows sin is going to end. He knows injustice, oppression, marginalization, and corruption are going to be erased. And he knows that with them will go all systems, all institutions, and all social conventions that perpetuate their cruelty on the earth.

But Daniel knows something more. He knows that when God brings an end to sin, anyone who clings to it, anyone who has identified themselves with its luxuries and exploitative scaffolds, will be destroyed along with it. God is bringing an end to sin and injustice. He is cleansing the universe. And anyone who clings to sins dark substance will be destroyed with it.

And Daniel knows one more thing: That his entire nation—the people of Israel—are in a mess. Their justice system is corrupt. Their politicians are chasing power. Their royal families are pursuing luxury and security. Their people are worshiping idols. Human trafficking (temple prostitution) and human sacrifice were taking place. Widows and orphans could be abused without justice. Bribery was common. And things got so bad that the story tells us the streets of Jerusalem flowed with the blood of the innocent (2 Kings 21:16).

So when Daniel sees the end of sin, the eradication of injustice and oppression, and the birth of a new reconstructed neighborhood of saints, he freaks out because he immediately thinks: *what will happen to Israel?*

In short, if God is about to cleanse reality of evil, what will happen to a nation steeped in evil? The question drives Daniel to despair.

Read Daniel 9:1–19
What is Daniel asking for in this prayer?

_____

_____

_____

Daniel prays this prayer some time after the vision of the cleansing of the sanctuary. You can sense his agony and fear. He fears that when God restores the cosmos, his people will not inhabit the new world. They are too fallen, and their injustice has placed them beyond the promise of a renewed society.

So Daniel prays and weeps. And as he prays, Gabriel shows up to give Daniel the solution (wohoo!) Gabriel says to him, "a period of time has been set aside for your people and your holy city," and in that period, there is a list of things you have to do in order to have a place in Creator's new world. Here's a simple breakdown:

1. Finish their rebellion
2. Put an end to their sin
3. Atone for their guilt
4. Bring in everlasting righteousness
5. Confirm the prophetic vision
6. Anoint the most holy

The simple breakdown is still confusing, so let's simplify it a bit more. The first two items on the list are pretty straight forward. Here are items 3-6:

3. Item three says they need to "atone" for their guilt. The word "atone" means to be "at-One." Guilt breaks oneness. Creator wants his people's guilt removed so they can be "at-one" with him again.

4. Item four says they need to bring in everlasting righteousness. The word righteousness simply means to be in a "right relationship." Creator wants his people to enter into a harmonious state of "right relationship" with him and each other.

5. The fifth point simply means that the vision being explored will come to pass.

6. And the sixth point goes back to the previous study on the cleansing of the sanctuary. It's kind of complicated, so we won't go into it here. But for now, it's enough to know that "anointing the most holy" is sanctuary language that basically means the plan of salvation is in motion.

Notice how most of this is salvation language. Israel had been in rebellion to God, but now they had another opportunity to enter into harmony with him. Gabriel basically says: *There is a solution to your worries Daniel. Israel just has to do these six things, and then voila! The nation can be a part of God's new world.*

But there's a problem: How could Israel possibly accomplish any of the tasks in that list? If God told you that in the next few months you had one more chance to do all those things, what would you do?

Chances are you would go into despair mode. There is just no way for a fallen human being, conditioned by sin all their life, to ever accomplish any of the tasks on that list—let alone all of them.

But the good news is, Gabriel's explanation doesn't end there. In the very next verse he tells Daniel that as the period of time transpired something amazing would happen, "a ruler—the Anointed One—comes" (25).

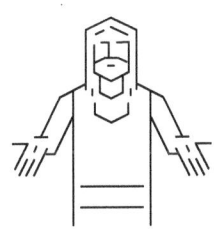

Enter Jesus

You can explore the rest of this vision—including the timeline, dates, history etc.—in the PDF linked via the QR code above (page 150). For now, we are going to focus on this "Anointed One" because, it turns out, everything points to him.

Read Luke 4:14–21
What does Jesus say about himself in this verse?

_____

_____

_____

Jesus declares that he is the "Anointed One" of God. In fact, the word "messiah" and "Christ"—both used as descriptors of Jesus—literally mean "anointed one." Hundreds of years before it took place, the angel Gabriel predicts the arrival of Jesus, the "Anointed One."

And here is where it gets good. It turns out that every, single item on the list Gabriel gave Daniel is fulfilled entirely by Jesus. Through his life, death, and resurrection, Jesus accomplished what no man could ever do. He:

1. Brought an end to rebellion
2. Conquered the power of sin
3. Atoned for Humanity's Separation
4. Brought in everlasting righteousness
5. Confirmed the prophetic vision
6. Anointed the most holy

We have already explored how Jesus accomplished this in part 1 of our journey. If you need a refresher, go back and read chapters 4 through 9. For now, here is the main point of Daniel's vision: *Everything God required of Israel, everything God desires for humanity, and everything God asks of any of us is completely and entirely fulfilled in Jesus.*

He is the One. He is the hero of the story. The birth of a new world, populated by a new humanity that moves to the rhythms of love, is found entirely in Jesus.

This means that, if you and I want to be a part of this new world in which true justice reigns—a world defined by relational oneness, a world in which sin no longer harasses—we only have to do one thing: Receive Jesus as the only one who can redeem, restore, and rebirth us into this new experience.

And the crazy part is that this gift of redemption is available, not only to the victims of injustice, but to its agents as well. This is the point of the vision! That there is hope for all of us. That there is a table for all of us. That all mankind, regardless of the dark pages of our past, are invited into redemption. This is why, nearly 700 years before his birth, another prophet—speaking of Jesus—could say:

He was despised and rejected—a man of sorrows, acquainted with deepest grief. We turned our backs on him and looked the other way. He was despised, and we did not care. Yet it was our weaknesses he carried; it was our sorrows that weighed him down. And we thought his troubles were a punishment from God, a punishment for his own sins!

But he was pierced for our rebellion, crushed for our sins. He was beaten so we could be whole. He was whipped so we could be healed (Isaiah 53: 2–6).

Read the rest of this Jesus-vision in Isaiah 53: 7–12.
What does this prophecy mean to you, personally?

_____
_____
_____
_____
_____
_____

If there was one way of summarizing the meaning of Daniel 9 for our modern age it would be this:

The global village we long for, the ecological harmony we seek, the social equity and justice we envision, and the reconstructed neighborhood of human civilization that we pursue will not be achieved through politics, technology, economics, or religion. This new world, this cosmos reborn, will come to be only through the promise of Jesus. And the table of this new world is open to all. Sinners and thieves, liars and culprits—there is a hope, a rebirth, and a new world for us all. And to those who believe, He becomes the way, the truth, and the life—the answer to the question, "How long?" and the birth of a new self, a new humanity, and a new world.

In him, everything is made new.

REFLECT

The vision is all about Jesus. By accepting him, the nation of Israel would have fulfilled everything required of them. And it's the same with each of us. Jesus is the fulfillment of all Creator requires. And this is the message of the church: that *Jesus is the way.* He is the solution to our brokenness and suffering. He is the answer to our heart-wrenching questions. In Jesus, the war between the two kingdoms will meet its end. By his death and resurrection, he overthrew the lies of the Satan and conquered the empire of self. In him, a new civilization, moving to the rhythms of love, begins and never ends.

CONNECT

Review _____
_____

Open _____
_____

Ask _____
_____

Decide _____
_____

ENGAGE

Scan the QR code to watch this chapter's accompanying Reflection video.

SCAN ME: THE ONE

7. THE PORTAL

In the previous chapter, we focused on the vision in Daniel 9—one of the most intense visions in the entire Bible. The central theme of the vision is Jesus. As a nation, Israel was invited to enter into the story of salvation that God was bringing to the world. Then, after the death and resurrection of Jesus, a new thing emerged. Christ gave birth to a new humanity, the continuation of Israel known as the church—a trans-national, multi-cultural, trans-human community centered in the new Adam, Jesus. Below is a quick summary of what we have seen so far:

Daniel 2

Empires at war against humanity and against God. Empires destroyed and forever replaced by a new kingdom.

Daniel 7

Empires at war against humanity and against God. The church-empire as the chief antagonist against God.

Daniel 8

The church-empire at war against God. Divine cosmic justice destroys it, along with all systems of oppression and sin. New kingdom begins.

Daniel 9

The key, center, portal, and foundation of this new kingdom, populated by a new humanity, is Jesus-only. In him, everything is made new.

Let's bring this all together. Daniel reveals the battle between good and evil that began in heaven, and has continued on the earth for thousands of years (Daniel 2). Eventually, the church itself was corrupted into an empire and became the Satan's main instrument of warfare against God (Daniel 7–8), spreading lies about him and perpetuating suffering on the earth.

A being then asks the key question: "How long will this go on?" (Daniel 8:13), and the angel responds: "there will be 2300 years then the sanctuary"—oneness with God—"will be restored" (Daniel 8:14)—a Hebrew metaphor of cosmic cleansing.

The vision ends shortly after and Daniel is confused. But in chapter 9, the angel Gabriel returns and says, "I have now come to give you wisdom and understanding..." (Daniel 9:22). As we saw in the previous chapter, the explanation Gabriel brings centers on one thing: *Jesus, the "One."*

But why Jesus? Isn't the suggestion, that he is the only way, exclusive and unkind? What about the hard work and creative spirit that humans have put toward healing the social issues of our world? The many religious ideologies, spiritual pathways, political systems, philosophical narratives, and technological advances? If we say Jesus is the only way, are we not being arrogant?

Why Jesus?

The easiest way to answer this question is with an illustration from the classic film franchise: *The Matrix*. If you have never seen any of the movies, here is a simple explanation of the plotline brought to you by our robotic overlord, ChatGPT:

The Matrix films are a set of science fiction movies that tell the story of a man named Neo who lives in a future world where people are controlled by advanced computers. In this world, people think they're living their normal lives, but in reality, their bodies are hooked up to machines and they're actually in a virtual reality called the Matrix.

Neo is recruited by a group of rebels who help him understand that the world he thought was real, isn't real at all. They also help him discover that he is "The One" meaning, he is a special kind of human who has special powers that he can use to fight against the machines. Together, Neo and the rebels go on a journey to try to free humanity.

However, here is the twist that changes everything. It turns out "The One" isn't really a savior. He is just another loop the machines have invented to keep humans in slavery to the matrix—designed to make them think they are fighting for freedom while controlling them at the same time.

Neo represents what all human efforts for salvation truly are: promises of liberation that always loop us back into the same system of injustice and violence. Because humanity exists within the matrix of sin, everything we engineer to get us out is still engineered within the matrix. In the end, all of our political revolutions, religious establishments, technological advances, and philosophical movements end the same way: back where we started, still trapped in the matrix of sin with its endless cycles of trauma.

The only way to escape such a cycle is if someone from outside the system enters in, defeats the system, and then shows us the way out. That someone is Jesus, who came from the Father, overcame the Satan, conquered the grave, and tore a whole in the fabric of sin's matrix, offering humanity the only way out in history. That way is not a new religion. That way is himself.

Step Through The Portal

Read John 10:9 and 14:6. Also, Acts 4:12
What do these verses mean in your own journey with God?

_____
_____
_____

Jesus identifies himself as the way, the door, and the gate. He is the portal out of the fallen system we inhabit and into a new humanity and a new world. In him, humanity is forever secure. Unlike the nihilistic theories that suggest the universe will eventually die and humanity's memory forever erased, Jesus shows us that in him our species will never, ever end.

But of course, the promise is better than mere eternal existence. The visions of Daniel show that, in Jesus, the universe will be cleansed. In a sense, its not just humans who step through the portal of Jesus and into a new reality—it is all of creation! The entire cosmos finds its rebirth in Jesus. And we see this clearly in the apocalyptic visions of the seer, Daniel.

The final judgment is God's last act to reverse sin and restore universal harmony.

All human empires (church included) are annihilated. The empire of self is destroyed.

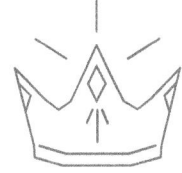

The kingdom is given to those who have embraced the way of love in Christ (the saints).

As we have seen, in the Old Testament, the cleansing of the sanctuary was a metaphor of cosmic cleansing. It represents the final phase of God's redemptive plan. According to the angel, before the story of rebellion ends, God enters this final phase of restoration. And when it ends, all things are made new.

How long will individual and collective humanity perpetuate lies about God? How long will we propagate bloodshed in the name of corporation, slavery in the name of expansion, disparity in the name of luxury, and exclusion in the name of religion? The cleansing points us to the promise that final redemption is nearly here. And the way through it, the portal to this new reality, is Jesus.

Before we close this chapter, I need to point out the visions of Daniel 8-9 are not yet complete. If you want to finish deciphering the timeline, you can do so with the PDF below. If timelines make you dizzy, feel free to skip to the final thoughts.

Scan here to download chapter supplement

SCAN ME: THE PORTAL

Final Thoughts

Before we close our time with these bizarre visions, one more point needs to be made. Their message is about so much more than apocalyptic foreshadowing. Instead, the realities they unveil call us to reorient our lives in very significant ways. Here are three primary invitations that the message of a present-day, cosmic judgment calls us toward:

I.

Because the church-empire engineered a counter-narrative filled with lies about God, the restoration of the sanctuary means that God is restoring the truth about himself. You and I are part of that final restoration that deconstructs the spiritual propaganda of the other horn and awakens humanity to the truth of God's character of love.

2.

Because human empire is built on the beastly impulse of self, the judgment demonstrates the reversal of all human empire and the injustice, oppression, and suffering they perpetuate. You and I are part of that reversal that resists the injustices deeply cemented and calcified in our societies. Regardless of our nationality, race, or culture, the judgment calls us to transcend all this by embracing the new humanity/society that we are in Christ and to live with allegiance to his kingdom above all things.

This means being willing to live counter-cultural lives and to reject and resist the patterns of coercion, control, and hate that dominate our social, religious, and cultural landscapes. In short, the cosmic judgment calls us to live as agents of reversal, rejecting the ways of fallen humanity by announcing the way of Christ's new humanity and his new kingdom to which we already belong.

3.

Finally, because the ultimate end of the judgment is the restoration of oneness in the universe, you and I are called to live lives of oneness here and now.

Eternity is not a future experience, it is a present reality. Eternal life begins the moment we enter into relationship with Jesus. And best of all, eternal life isn't about how long we live, but how well we live. In short, eternity is a quality of life, not just a quantity. And that quality of life—a life governed by the rhythms of love and relational oneness—begins the moment we receive Christ and his spirit begins to flow through our own. Jesus said the kingdom of heaven is in us already (Luke 17:21), so as the cosmic judgment demolishes the empires of man, we are called to live out the tempos of the kingdom in the here and now.

In living out the truth of who God is—by revealing his character to the world; participating in the reversal of empire by living in harmony with love, not self; and by manifesting oneness with God and others in the here and now—we participate in what God is doing in the cosmos.

In the next chapter, we will explore what this divine-human participation looks like in more detail. Until then, meditate and discuss the following text with your fellow travelers:

The day of the Lord will come
unexpectedly like a thief in the night;
and on that day, the sky will vanish with a roar,
the elements will melt with intense heat, and
the earth and all the works done on it will be
seen as they truly are. Knowing that one day
all this will come to pass, think what sort of
people you ought to be—how you should be
living faithful and godly lives, waiting
hopefully for and hastening the coming of
God's day when the heavens will vanish in
flames and the elements melt away with
intense heat. What will happen next, and what
we hope for, is what God promised: a new
heaven and a new earth
where justice reigns.

2 Peter 3:10–13, (The Voice)

HEALING TEACHING

Some religious traditions teach that God predetermined everything that happens. This means the Satan's rebellion and our consequent sufferings are all part of his grand cosmic script playing itself out. Such despotic ideas demonstrate how effective the Satan has been at co-opting the Bible in order to paint a cruel picture of God that causes us to fear rather than trust him. The truth is, God is not the cause of sin or suffering. He is its cure.

REFLECT

Soon, the empire of man will collapse, never to rise again. Where does our allegiance lie? If we say we are part of the eternal kingdom of love, then this can only mean one thing—that as God performs his work of judgment over the injustices of man's fallen empire in heaven, his people on earth will dedicate all that they are to the reversal of suffering, injustice, and lies about God. Through acts of service, humanitarian justice, and the spread of the gospel, we live out the Kingdom of God on earth while preparing the way for its beautifully catastrophic arrival, described in Daniel 2 as the stone that grinds the history of empire into powder. In short, the visions call you and I to live lives in opposition to man's selfish kingdom. In doing so, we prepare the way for the arrival of a new kingdom, built not on the beastly impulse of self, but on the eternal ethic of agape love.

CONNECT

Review _____
_____

Open _____
_____

Ask _____
_____

Decide _____
_____

ENGAGE

Scan the QR code to watch this chapter's accompanying Reflection video.

SCAN ME: THE PORTAL

8. THE PROTEST

Daniel's visions revealed the rise and fall of four major empires, with the fourth (Rome) experiencing a political fracturing that lasts to this day. In the aftermath of this collapse, we were introduced to the "other horn," which represented the church-empire. During the church's 1000+ year rule, the visions depict a time where lies about God, spiritual abuse, and injustice would dominate the human experience. However, the visions also disclose that at the set time God would bring human history and empire into judgment. The vision of the cleansing points us to that time and marks the beginning of the end of all exploitative, man-made systems. We are in that time now—the age of judgment—in which God overturns the lies about himself and deconstructs the pillars of corporation and power. This restoration of truth (sanctuary restored) will take place and usher in a new kingdom.

The question—"How long?..."—of Daniel 8:14 has been answered, not with precise numbers, but with a story. A story in which God has drawn a line in the sand and said, "no more." Soon, the suffering that prompted that question—perpetuated by the beastly empires of man and perfected by the church-empire itself—will come to an end. A new civilization, fueled by love unconditional, will populate the earth.

So then, where does the story go from here? As we saw in the previous lesson, the realization that we are living in the final chapter of human history, and that, right now, God is engaged in the process of judgment against the institutions and governmental structures of this world, has serious implications. For starters, this reality confronts our political commitments, our economic priorities, and our individual ideals. Political because every system we support is currently being weighed for destruction. Economic because what we do with our resources and privileges depends on which kingdom we belong to. Individual because the Kingdom of God demands our all, and it's agape foundation calls us to reorient everything in our lives.

There is certainly more that this reality of a present-time judgment confronts us with. However, to keep things simple, we are only going to focus on the largest themes already present in the visions of Daniel, and which we have already touched on in previous lessons. The first is the revelation of God's heart. The second is the reversal of the Satan's empire.

A Revelation of God's Heart

As we have already seen, God's character is revealed all throughout scripture. That revelation, however, finds its greatest clarity at the cross. Without the cross, all other biblical themes are mere concepts. But with the cross, each of them become deeply personal. Let's explore this a bit more in the following verses:

Genesis 3:15; Hebrews 2:14; and Colossians 2:14–15. How does their message relate to our personal lives and the human story as a whole?

_____

_____

_____

The cross defeated the Satan. It forever proved that he was a liar and that God is love. The whole universe then knew the truth about Lucifer's government. But not the people on Earth. Apart from a few hundred Jesus followers, no one understood the magnitude of what had just happened. In fact, not many people outside of Jerusalem had any clue that anything significant had even happened in the first place! Thus, with Israel's official rejection of Christ, the early Christian church was born. And it was now, via the church, that God would flood the earth with the truth about himself.

But as we have already seen, rather than an ocean of spiritual truth, the church-empire brought decades of spiritual drought. And on the heels of a distorted picture of God, the church came to instigate and justify centuries of political subterfuge and spiritual abuse. But this would not go on forever. Not only did the church meet a political end during the French Revolution, but Daniel reveals that God himself will destroy her forever. The final judgment then marks the beginning of the end of the meta-rival's war against God. During this era, the church—which represents the apex of human empire—and indeed all self-centered regimes, will meet an eternal and irreversible conclusion.

However, there is one problem. As we saw in the previous chapter (and explored in more detail in the PDF downloads), this judgment is administered in a mysterious, trans-terrestrial sanctuary that none of us can see. Therefore, if God is going to restore the truth about himself and deconstruct human empire before the judgment ends, he needs to do something radical on the earth that synchronizes with the cleansing of the cosmic sanctuary.

WOMAN/MALE CHILD

- The Church
  (2 Corinthians 11:2)
- Gives Birth, Male Child is Jesus, taken by God (Acts 1)
- Church Flees from Dragon/Rome and hides
- God sustains her for 1260 Days

DRAGON

- 7 Heads and 10 Horns (Daniel 7)
- The Satan, Rome, and Church war against God
- Tries to kill Jesus, Persecutes the church
- Fails, Angry with the church, Attacked her children

Turn to the New Testament book of Revelation. Read chapter 12 and pay special attention to verse 16.

As usual, the details of the vision can be dizzying. There is a woman, a child, a dragon, stars, and what appears to be spirit-realm chaos unfolding. How can we make sense of this?

A simple description that harmonizes with the story we have explored so far goes like this: The woman in the vision represents the church, and the male child is Jesus. The dragon is none other than the Satan, whose lies caused one-third of the angels in heaven to fall with him. The dragon also represents the terrifying beast of Daniel—church-empire—with Lucifer being the mastermind behind both. In the vision, the dragon tries to destroy Jesus but fails, so it turns its attention to the church. And it is here, in Revelation, that we are introduced to two churches—the church-empire and its alternative, the underground church.

The underground church, represented by a mystical woman, flees into the wilderness where she is protected for 1260 days/years (the same period of time in Daniel in which the church-empire ruled and warred against God). When the

Satan sees that all of his attempts to destroy the underground church have failed, he is furious. During the 1260 years of papal rule, divergents were persecuted and killed. The church-empire did everything it could, but the underground church was protected.

Then, something remarkable happened. Toward the end of its reign, as the church-empire began to lose its political grip, a protest emerged. A monk named Martin Luther discovered what we have been exploring all along: that salvation is a gift of God that cannot be earned. Soon after Luther's rediscovery of the narrative of salvation, he began protesting the church's abuses and corruption and calling everyone back to the narrative of God's heart, revealed in scripture.

Read the following verses: Romans 5:6–10; 1 Peter 3:18; and 1 Peter 2:24–25. What do they say about the cross and what meaning do you think they would have had for Luther?

_____

_____

_____

Luther's rediscovery of the cross spawned a global protest and return to the heart of the father. But the struggle was far from over. As the underground church re-emerged in resistance to the church-empire's injustices, many went on to replicate those same injustices. Church tribes were formed, and some united with state powers to enforce their ideas with the threat of capital punishment. Even to this day, Christianity is known globally as a political power with a political agenda. Those who don't fit the agenda experience oppression, and, in turn, the false perception of God as tyrant is perpetuated on the earth.

What this means on a practical level then is that, despite the growth and spread of the church, lies about God abound. And if there is one thing God will and must accomplish before his return, it is a full and total revelation of his heart of love. Without this revelation, people cannot make informed decisions about him. So the task is set before us: Everyone must know who he really is and what he is really like. This is why Jesus declared that he would only return when the good news of the kingdom was proclaimed to the whole earth. The spell of lies must be broken, the political propaganda of the Satan must be exposed, and everyone must be given the chance to know for themselves what God is really like.

Reversal of The Satan's Empire

A revelation of God's heart, however, cannot revolve merely around talking and teaching theology. Rather, the Bible tells us that there is a way that—when combined with scriptures narrative—opens the eyes of the world to the character of God. Read the following verses and summarize what they are calling us to: Through the practical harmonizing of sharing the gospel, meaningful social action, and the pursuit of humanitarian justice, God's people become agents of reversal whose daily lives protest the empire of the Satan by living out the agape-love patterns of God's eternal kingdom.

Isaiah 1:17

_____

_____

Matthew 5:16

_____

_____

Proverb 31:8–9

_____

_____

John 15:8,12

_____

_____

Psalm 82:3

_____

_____

Matthew 25:35–40

_____

_____

This assignment has always belonged to the church, but today, as we live in the final phase of the story, the call is even more urgent. The church-empire cast a spell of lies over human civilization. These lies dominate the cultural consciousness and form the prime basis for how many of us think about and relate to God. This beastly illusion is so strong that even those who emerged from the underground to protest the injustices of the church were lured by its promise of power and control. History recounts the tragic results, and our contemporary age bears witness to the church's continued thirst for power.

However, God is not done yet. He has a people on the earth, a new humanity, a redeemed and restored species that belongs, not to the first Adam who allied himself to the serpent but to the second Adam who crushed the serpent's head.

These people, of this new species of human, are the true people of God. They are a transhuman community, not because they are a fusion of man and machine but are a synthesis of man and divinity. In Jesus, fully God and fully man then, a new humanity is born—what author Ty Gibson refers to as "Humanity 2.0"—that moves, not to the selfish impulse of self but to the rhythms of eternal love. And it is through the presence of Jesus in this people, this new humanity, that the truth about God's heart of love will be restored on the earth.

HEALING TEACHING

During the age of the church-empire, the very story of scripture was colonized and reinterpreted in ways that benefited the institutions economic and political growth. It was during this time that many of the dogmas that fuel religious trauma were anchored in the church's identity. Religious trauma and spiritual abuse then are systemic issues engineered by an empire at war against God.

REFLECT

By corrupting the church, the Satan tried to destroy God's truth. He was given over 1000 years to do so, yet, in the midst of this, the underground church emerged out of the wilderness to flood the world with the real story of who God is and what he is like. The church-empire fell, further opening the way for the narrative of Gods heart to advance. But the influence of its propaganda machine was too strong. In time, even those protesting its injustices went on to perpetuate them. But there is still hope. The judgment phase of the redemption story is here, and in this final phase, God will demolish empire and usher in his new kingdom—a world populated, not by fallen humanity but by a new humanity in harmony with God's own heart of love.

CONNECT

Review ___

Open ___

Ask ___

Decide ___

ENGAGE

Scan the QR code to watch this chapter's accompanying Reflection video.

SCAN ME: THE PROTEST

9. THE REMAINING

Nearly a thousand years after Daniel, another prophet, named John, was given a series of intense images about future events. These events were recorded in the book of Revelation, which we are now exploring. The previous chapter dove into Revelation 12, which unfolds the narrative of the church's oppressive reign using the images of a woman (representing the underground church) and a dragon (representing the church-empire). This is basically the same plotline of Daniel 7–8, but while Daniel focused most of his attention on the church-empire, John placed most of his attention on the church-underground.

Read the following texts to see the parallels. Then, we will explore the meaning of the underground church and what its relevance is in the war between good and evil.

Daniel 7:25
Church-empire

He will speak out against the Most High and wear down the saints of the Highest One...and they will be given into his hand for a time, times, and half a time.

Revelation 12:13-14
Underground Church

He persecuted the woman...But the two wings of the great eagle were given to the woman, so that she could fly into the wilderness to her place, where she was nourished for a time and times and half a time, from the presence of the serpent.

Let's add some color to this picture. The Satan worked via Rome and church-empire to destroy the narrative of God's heart and his church. However, God led his church underground to protect it during its 1000+ years of tyranny. Then, as its time drew to a close, a monk named Martin Luther spawned a protest through which the underground church re-emerged. The church-empire was powerless to stop the movement. Truth was making a comeback and this caused the archnemesis to become enraged. John writes:

> *So the dragon was enraged with the woman, and went off to make war with the rest of her children, who keep the commandments of God and hold to the testimony of Jesus (Revelation 12:17).*

So here is our question for today. Why does any of this empire vs underground church stuff matter? To answer this question, we have to pause the story and take a dive into Revelation 12:17. By the time we are done, the contemporary relevance of the underground vs church-empire will make perfect sense.

War

John says the dragon "went off to make war." The Greek word for war is polemos, which can also be understood as a "dispute" (we get the word polemics from it). In other words, this war is not a physical war, but a war of ideas and words—a dispute over the character of God. This is what the battle between good and evil has always been about and it continues to our very day. The church-empire played a central role in this war, but while it lost its power, its influence did not fade.

What this means is that the church-empire is not merely an institution, it is an idea. Because ideas don't have borders, we can avoid being a part of the institutional church-empire and belong to it nonetheless if we hold to and promote false ideas about God's character. This calls us to place our emphasis, not on the corporate identity of the church-empire but on the characteristics of the underground church and the story it tells.

Leftovers

The second point to note is that the dragon's war has a target. And that target is the "rest of her"—the underground church's—"children." Another way of putting it is this: the Satan's end-time target is the "leftovers" of the underground church, or that which remains. According to John, this meta-rival saw that he had failed to destroy the underground church, so he makes war with what is left over of that community. This is an important point to note because the war is not about political conspiracies (government or administrative secrets) or national tension (this nation versus that nation). While those things will certainly take place, Lucifer's target is not any particular nation or society, but anyone and everyone who clings to the truth about God's character.

Seed

The final point to note is that the Satan's war against the leftovers of the underground church is not a war against an organization. John goes on to use the Greek word "seed" to define what the leftovers represent. The seed of the underground church is made of all those who cling faithfully to the truth of who God is. In the same way that falsehood is about ideas, truth is also about ideas. The seed of the true church is not institutional—it doesn't have a tax number or a corporate logo. Rather, it is anyone who clings to the story of God's character of love.

Let's bring it all together now. The dragon's war against God failed, and his main tool of warfare—the church-empire—fell. The underground church spread into the world with the story of the cross and, for the first time in decades, truth began to re-emerge. But the many churches that formed in the aftermath of the re-emergence began to pursue power and control as well. Tragically, the same injustices of the church-empire were repeated. Slavery, the displacement and genocide of native and indigenous peoples, racism, sexism, and more are just some of the heartbreaking injustices perpetuated by influential Christian institutions. On the heels of these developments, the promise of a cosmic judgment that sets everything right marks the beginning of the end of empire. In this judgment, God calls his people to the deconstruction and dismantling of their systemic inequities and to the manifestation of true love on the earth.

But the enemy, enraged and knowing his time is short, goes forth to make war once again. And as we have already seen, the Satan always wages war primarily through ideology that corrupts. So, it should come as no surprise to us that the church often manifests the very evils of empire. However, the story isn't over. John goes on to describe a people who resist the Satan's lure of empire and gives two identifying characteristics of them. Go back and read them in Revelation 12:17.

> *So the dragon was enraged with the woman, and went off to make war with the rest of her children,*
>
> *...who keep the commandments of God*
>
> *...and hold to the testimony of Jesus (Revelation 12:17).*

Keep His Commandments

John gives us two descriptions. The first is that the children of the underground church are those who "keep the commandments of God." But what does keeping God's commandments mean?

Read the following texts and discuss their relevance here: Matthew 22:34–40, 23:23, Romans 13:10

_____

_____

_____

Keeping God's commandments has nothing to do with being a hyper-strict, religious prude. God's law is a law of love. Therefore, to keep his law is synonymous with living a life in synchronicity with his heart of love. This means that the underground church is a movement that can be identified by its pursuit of God's heart. It is a people engaged in a harmonious walk with the divine heart and each other.

Have the Testimony of Jesus

John mentions one more identifying characteristic of the underground church. Not only do they live in harmony with the law of love, but they have the "testimony of Jesus."

Read Revelation 12:11 and 19:10. How do these verses help us understand what the "testimony of Jesus" is?

_____

_____

_____

There are two simple ways of understanding the meaning of the phrase "testimony of Jesus."

One is our testimony about Jesus and the other is Jesus's testimony about himself. Revelation 12:11 points to our personal experience with Jesus. Revelation 19:10 shows us that Jesus also has a testimony about himself, and that testimony is revealed in prophecy. So, John's meaning is clear: the Spirit of Prophecy is the testimony of Jesus. That is, the prophetic visions present a narrative that lifts Jesus up. Therefore, the leftovers of the underground church are a tribe that both live out the love of God and embrace the prophetic narrative that exalts Jesus through the entirety of earth's story.

He is the way and he alone.

Why Does Any of it Matter?

Now we get to the "why it matters" part. The Satan's war against God is a war of ideas. Through the influence of the historic church, the false ideas live on. The underground church re-enters the story as the restorer of truth during the final phase of the war (judgment/cleansing of the sanctuary). But that restoration of truth takes place in a specific way, which is best explained using the following illustration:

Imagine a ballet dancer performing before an audience. The dancer is graceful, talented, and inspiring to watch. But something amazing happens when a second dancer enters the stage and the two perform a harmonious and interconnected dance together. Somehow, the beauty of the lone dancer is enhanced by the arrival of a partner. This illustration helps us understand John's point in Revelation. Our personal testimony united with Jesus's prophetic testimony of himself creates a harmonious dance of truth. Its not one or the other, but both.

The underground church is a community of people engaged in a harmonious dance between God's prophetic revelation and their personal experience with him. It is via this means that true ideas about God are restored to the world.

John's vision matters because we are each called to be a part of this restoration of truth, by a personal experience with God and a proclamation of Jesus's prophetic self-revelation.

This harmonious dance began when the underground church re-emerged, and continues to this day. Through it, the truth of God's character of love is being revealed. As the church engages, the culture tells a personal and prophetic story. Together, these two narratives melt into the minds and hearts of people everywhere, delivering them from the lies of the Satan and into a redemptive relationship with God. You and I are a part of that personal and prophetic revelation to the world.

Prophecy is Protest

However, there is one more element to Jesus's prophetic voice that needs to be understood and embraced. As we have seen all throughout Daniel, and now in Revelation, prophecy is not just promise, but protest. In other words, the prophetic voice opposes the unjust systems and structures of temporal human power. In doing so, prophecy calls humanity to more than mere knowledge of future events. It calls us to place all our allegiance with Christ, as king, and abdicate all temporal, man-made, nationalistic loyalties, in order to live out the ethic of oneness and love in a world of division and self-interest.

This call to protest is rooted in God's sanctuary-heart and redemptive plan, and moves us to speak up for the voiceless and against corruption and unfairness. This is all done while proclaiming—not a new political philosophy—but a new kingdom, rooted and grounded in the self-sacrifice of Christ its king.

As we close part 2, read the words of the prophet Isaiah 1:1–17. What is God's message through him, and how does it impact your own life and faith?

_____

_____

_____

HEALING TEACHING

The anti-God propaganda engineered by the church-empire continues to be the primary way through which most people today see and understand God. But the story of Jesus continues to be the prime antidote. As we explore his way, we get to know his heart and it liberates us from the spell of lies the church-empire has cast over the earth.

REFLECT

The Satan waged a war against Israel by corrupting it, but out of Israel came the church. With clever ideological subterfuge, the meta-rival corrupted it as well. During the church's years of dominance, he tried to erase the narrative of God's heart, not by deleting it but by rewriting it. But God is never caught by surprise. He had a plan all along. Through the ancient protesters down to our contemporary age, the God-story of scripture lives on. God has always had a bunch of leftovers who stubbornly cling to his heart. The final battle is soon to come, but the track record has been set. Love *always* wins.

CONNECT

Review _____
_____

Open _____
_____

Ask _____
_____

Decide _____
_____

ENGAGE

Scan the QR code to watch this chapter's accompanying Reflection video.

SCAN ME: THE REMAINING

PIT STOP

Congratulations on finishing part two of The Road! By now, you will have learned the overarching story of the Bible, from God/Creation to Restoration and into the narrative of the church-empire—from the time the Bible closed until the present day. The battle between good and evil didn't end when Jesus died on the cross. It continues with the church itself, emerging the main antagonist in the story. But God has never allowed the truth about himself to be completely wiped out, so even today, his true *ecclesia* emerges to reveal to the world his heart of love. You are a part of that community!

In part 3, we are going to peel back the layers of mystery and unravel the final chapters of the story. You will encounter visions of a time yet to be, events yet to occur, and tensions yet to emerge. But overall, you will catch a glimpse of a world we have yet to know; where we will live forever in restored community with God.

But before we get into that, we need to make sure that the foundation is set so that what is to come is built on what you have already seen. So we are due for another pit stop. Again, the purpose of the pit stop is to go back to the beginning to refresh, refine, and reinforce what we have learned. Use the instructions below and discuss the points with your fellow travelers. By the end of this pit stop you should have a solid foundation for the rest of the journey. Let's get started!

SCAN ME: PART 2 PIT STOP

REFRESH

The War

As beautiful as the gospel is, there is a darker side to the story. The Satan hates God, God's people, and—most of all—the gospel. Consequently, he seeks to confuse, distort, and—if possible—conceal the good news of God's love for humanity. His power is in the lies he tells—lies about God. Because the church is the means by which God reveals his true identity to the world, the dragon has waged a war against it just as he did with the people of Israel in the Old Testament.

The Empires

Daniel, the "seer," saw a cosmic struggle between two kingdoms. One kingdom is the kingdom of men, ruled by selfishness. The other is the Kingdom of God, ruled by love. This heavenly kingdom is yet to be seen, and it is a kingdom that, according to Daniel, "will never end." Unlike human empires, this kingdom will last because it is built on the rhythm of love rather than the impulse of self.

The Beast

A few decades after the last of the apostles died, the church morphed into a religio-political empire. The gospel was distorted into a system of religious rituals, grace was erased, and the story of God replaced by a counter-narrative that misrepresented his character until he was barely recognizable. The serpent's lies in Eden had now infiltrated the church and became its narrative.

The Other

Through the influence of the church-empire, the law of God was changed from a law of design, based on God's character of love, to an arbitrary law imposed by an authoritarian deity. Consequently, the church—also an authoritarian entity—showcased its power by arbitrarily changing the laws of God as a sign of its authority. This same oppressive nature was reflected in the church's political rule as well. The world now came to believe that God was a punitive, controlling, and distant deity. The sanctuary narrative was erased. The love of God was obscured. And the story Jesus came to tell replaced by a counter-narrative that painted God in repulsive and frightening colors.

The Reset

The war between justice and oppression won't go on forever. God has appointed a day for judgment to begin. The oppressive rule of kings and nations, along with the deceptions of the fallen church and every other system that has aligned itself with the enemy of love, will come to an end. The people of God will be delivered, and a new kingdom that operates in harmony with God's character will emerge, never to be replaced.

The One

Jesus is the center of scripture's judgment narrative. He is the solution to our brokenness and suffering. He is the answer to our heart-wrenching questions. In Jesus, the war between the two kingdoms will meet its end. By his death and resurrection, he overthrew the lies of the Satan and conquered the empire of self.

The Portal

This war is soon to end. But until then, Jesus resides in heaven's sanctuary where he is now engaged in his final act as judge. And from that same sanctuary, which communicates his eternal desire to dwell with us, he works tirelessly to bring this war to its end, so that we can once again be reunited with him. He is restoring the universe back to its original design. Soon, the suffering perpetuated by the beastly empires of man will come to an utter end, and a new kingdom ruled by love—unconditional and pure—will rule for eternal ages.

The Protest

By corrupting the church, the Satan tried to destroy God's truth. The church-empire fell, but its influence was too strong. In time, even those who protested its injustices went on to perpetuate them. But there is still hope. The judgment phase of the redemption story has been promised, and in this final phase, God will demolish empire and usher in his new kingdom—a world populated by a new humanity in harmony with God's own heart of love.

The Remaining

Lucifer waged a war against Israel by corrupting it, but out of Israel came the church. The Satan corrupted it as well, and for over 1000 years he tried to drown the true church. But God is never caught by surprise. He had a plan all along. Through the ancient protesters, down to our contemporary age, the God-story of scripture lives on. God has always had a bunch of leftovers who stubbornly cling to his narrative. The final battle is soon to come, but the track record has been set. *Love always wins.*

REFINE

The War	*What is the war between good and evil all about? (Hint: The Greek word for War in Revelation 12 is "polemos," from where we get our modern word "polemics," or "dispute.")*
The Empires	*Why do human empires always fail? Why is Gods eternal? (Hint: The foundation of human empire differs from the foundation of God's kingdom.)*
The Beast	*Daniel predicts an empire that would war against God like no other. Which empire was he referring to? (Hint: It started out as religious, not political.)*
The Other	*In what way did the church-empire war against God?*
Thr Reset	*How does God respond to this war against him and his government?*
The One	*Who is the center of God's judgment?*
The Portal	*What role does Jesus play in the final judgment? What does this mean for us individually?*
The Protest	*The lies the Satan told via the church met their end. How did this happen?*
The Remaining	*Even though the church was corrupted, God has a group of people who always remain faithful to his heart. Who are they? What is their identity?*

REINFORCE

In the overarching narrative of scripture, we have learned that there are 5 keys needed to unlock its full meaning. As we close part 2, there is a new key that we need to add. This key highlights that, all through scripture, God's self-revelation points us to a protest of injustice and human empire. Recognizing this "Protest" theme in scripture allows us to derive applicatory meaning from its story that can be manifested relevantly in our world today.

Trinity	*God is an eternal community of agape love.*
The Sanctuary	*God dwells "with" us in time and history.*
Design	*God's universe is built on other-centered parameters.*
Rebellion	*God is at war with the Satan and his selfish empire.*
Redemption	*God saves us through the gift of Jesus's sacrifice.*
Protest	*God reverses fallen empire through lives of protest.*

PART 3:
1. THE SIGN

In this final leg of our road trip, we are going to hone in on the final steps God is going to take to bring his redemptive plan full circle, with the birth of a new cosmos in harmony with his heart of love. The necessity of this redemptive aim is evident when we survey the history of human empire—replete with injustice, oppression, discrimination, and driven by an insatiable lust for power. But these are all mere symptoms of the beastly impulse of self that governs our fallen civilization and stand as evidence that humanity's kingdom is crumbling, burdened by the spell of sin that steers its every move. But the good news is a new creation is coming—the complete restoration of a universe that moves to the rhythms of love. This new creation is the Kingdom of God that Jesus came to reveal.

However, the very notion of redemption isn't exactly popular. Many today insist humanity doesn't need to be saved. But a quick scan of our own contemporary age suggests the opposite. Our world today is in a race against its own vulnerability and self-destruction. Whether its the environmental movement seeking to save the planet from corporate exploitation and bio-extinction, the social justice activists working to save society from inbuilt systemic injustices, plans to build a city on Mars in order to secure humanities continued survival, gene-editing, trans-humanism (blending man with machine), or neopolitical movements aimed at bringing about a new world order of equity one thing is clear—the human species recognizes that something is broken and that fixing it is a matter of existential survival. In short: *we need redemption.*

Jesus also has a plan of redemption. But it doesn't revolve around evolutionary, technological, or religio-political advancements. Jesus's redemptive plan is instead centered on the rebirthing of a whole new humanity from the old. According to Jesus, the real problem humanity faces is not educational, psychological, governmental or economic, our real problem is that we are a species who exist in separation from God, the only source of true agape love. In this state of separation, we find ourselves detached from the fountain of other-centered love, and this, in turn, gives birth to hearts driven by selfishness, the root of inequality, injustice, and beastly empires that mass-produce wealth for some and oppression for others. With this divine-human separation at play, such endemic suffering will never end.

In order to heal this chasm and restore us to the way of love, Jesus (who is God) became a human being and lived a life in unbroken oneness with the Father. In doing so, Jesus manifested a new kind of human—a spiritual, transhuman fusion of humanity and divinity. With his victory over death, the ultimate act of separation, Jesus promised to restore us to eternal oneness with God and, with this new humanity he has perfected in himself, to recreate us in his image of divine-human synchronicity.

In short, Jesus is humanity at its best, humanity in harmony with love; he aims now to restore us to unbroken oneness with God through himself, and, in turn, to birth a whole new humanity patterned after his self-abandoning love.

This Edenic restoration is intended to begin with the church—a community of people who are collectively the "new humanity"—called out from the way of self to the way of Christ. But what happens when the church itself becomes an empire and begins to perpetuate the very injustices and lies it is meant to resist? As we saw in the visions of Daniel, God saw the corruption of the church long before it was born. And according to the same visions, the church-empire—along with every other unjust human empire—will be judged and destroyed, and the earth will be given to a new people, a new society whom the angel refers to as "the people of the most-high" or "the saints." These are simply poetic ways of referring to a neospecies of humans whose life force flows from the heart of Jesus. So, this new human named Jesus is the king of a new kingdom and father of a new humanity rebirthed in his image. And it is this kingdom that we'll focus on in this final leg of our journey.

Before we dive in, however, one important point needs to be made. So far, everything we have studied has come to pass. The insights explored in Part 2 of this book spanned from the time of Babylon to the Industrial Age, leaving us in the our modern age—the time when the cosmic judgment was set to begin. However, the foresight's we will now explore have not taken place yet. So, get ready. Because in this final leg, we are traveling forward through time.

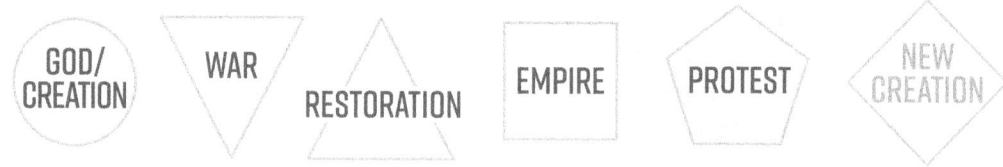

Prophecy As a Time Machine

As we step into our prophetic time machine, one thing will become clear. The center of what lies ahead is no different to the center of what lies behind: *God's heart of love*. In other words, just as Jesus is the aim of the past and present, he remains the aim of the future. Therefore, we will begin our journey by taking a leap into the future scenes of Jesus's return.

Read Matthew 24:3–12 and write down the signs Jesus mentions below:

_____
_____
_____
_____
_____
_____
_____

Notice the progression in the story:

False Christs/Deception → Wars and threats of war → Famines and earthquakes → Believers arrested, persecuted and killed → Hated all over the world → Many will turn away → Sin rampant, love will grow cold

Of course, none of these signs are strange or new. All of these things have been happening since sin entered the world. But remember; Jesus referred to these signs as "birth pains," and just like birth pains increase in frequency and intensity, so will each of these signs become more frequent and intense as the clock on human history reaches its final hour.

Nevertheless, notice something interesting: After predicting a time of intense "lies" (propaganda) about God and the rise in wars, Jesus says, "it's not the end yet" (v6). Then, after describing political instability, more war, and disasters, Jesus once again says, "it's still not the end" (v8). Then, he predicts persecution, apostasy, and more deception, but he still doesn't say it's the end. So then, when will the end come?

There is one more sign—the most important one—left to explore. Go back to Matthew 24 and read verses 12–14. What is the final sign that brings the end?

Notice the huge emphasis placed on lovelessness and love. The world will reach a state of utter lovelessness, but in the midst of this, there will be some who love persistently. This relentless love will lead them to continue spreading the gospel to a world dominated by hate and oppression. It is then that Jesus says, "the end will come."

The war of the two kingdoms explored in Daniel's vision continues to the end, with love and selfishness at constant war. But according to Jesus, love wins. And the final sign, the sign that his coming and is almost here, isn't war, political instability, or social pandemonium—it is a new humanity, a new community and a people who love like Jesus loves. In short, love—not hate—is the prelude to the kingdom.

The New Humanity

Think of it this way. When Jesus lived on the earth, he was God in human flesh. As a man, Jesus lived unlike any other human before or since. He was the only human to ever live in perfect love, harmoniously interconnected to the divine heart, rhythmically defined by other-centered compassion, and he moved with a posture of humility, servanthood, and grace. No other human has ever lived in such synchronicity with love like Jesus has. In a sense, he is a new kind of human—a spiritual transhuman as noted earlier—in whom divinity and humanity blend perfectly.

But it doesn't end there. Jesus then calls the church "his body"—an extension of himself—and connects us to himself so that his new humanity can flow through our old humanity and rebirth it, from selfishness to other-centered love. This is the grand mystery of scripture, the new thing God is doing, and the final sign that his kingdom is nearly here.

In Jesus, fallen humanity can transcend its "fallenness" and enter into a new dimension of being defined, not by the impulse of self but by the rhythms of agape love.

Reframing Apocalyptic Trauma

This perspective is essential, not only for its existential significance in our contemporary age but for its healing power. For decades, modern Christianity has perpetuated an apocalyptic obsession that borders on spiritual abuse. The messaging is always cynical, depressive, and focused on evil rather than good. The results of this kind of approach to the Bible's vision of "last things" is debilitating anxiety for some and emotional despair for others.

But, by revisiting scripture's end time visions from the angle of Christ's new humanity, we are invited to see that the apocalypse isn't about "end times" but, rather, the birthing of a new time. And it's not about what evil is up to, bizarre conspiracies, or doom and gloom predictions. To the contrary, it's about what love is up to.

And love, it turns out, is up to something beautiful.

REFLECT

The war of the two kingdoms continues to the end of time. But Jesus has promised that he will return, and that his kingdom will bring an end to all the empires of this world. The signs of his, soon, return are everywhere, and they are hints that we are nearing that time. But one sign has yet to be fulfilled—a people filled with radical love who spread the Jesus-story everywhere they go. This spiritual underground is so consumed by the agape love of God that even in the midst of oppression they continue to tell the story. And as they do, the final events are triggered, culminating in the arrival of the Kingdom of God.

CONNECT

Review _____

_____

Open _____

_____

Ask _____

_____

Decide _____

_____

ENGAGE

Scan the QR code to watch this chapter's accompanying Reflection video.

SCAN ME: THE SIGN

2. THE COLLAPSE

In the last chapter, we saw that the end of the rebellion story would come as a result of the love that God's people pour into the world—including their enemies. This unconditional love will catapult the gospel into all the nations, resulting in the return of Jesus. His return will mark the beginning of a new era in which love is once again the uncontested rhythm of life and being.

However, all is not perfect just yet. Before this happens, Jesus was clear that empire would face one final catastrophic collapse. In the midst of this collapse, the underground church would be hated, persecuted, and killed because of its allegiance to his kingdom over the empires of man. When and how these things will happen is something we don't know. But what we do know is that this social catastrophe will bring with it all the intolerance that the arch-nemesis has mastered through the centuries. The ecclesia will become *public enemy number one* and the hate-focus for those who have chosen to fuel their heart with the impulse of self instead of agape love.

When exploring this vision of the future, many people wonder how it's possible for our civilized society to ever embrace such a violation of human rights. Are we not more enlightened, educated, and cultured than ever before? How can we possibly get to such a low place? Only two points need to be established. First, while it may seem unlikely today, prophecy has shown us that God's predictions are always accurate. Things that seemed very unlikely when predicted happened just as written, time and time again. Second, society is a fickle thing. We can never count on it remaining the same forever. All it takes is one major upheaval for the selfish instinct to take over. Civilized as we may think we are, take away our economy, our food, or our shelter for a prolonged period of time and the self-interested instinct of sin and empire will wipe away all our civility.

So, what will this social collapse be like and how can we be among those who will love to the end? Those are the two questions we will now explore.

What Will this Social Collapse Be Like?

First it is important to note that this coming catastrophe will not emerge in a vacuum. It will emerge out of the collision of political and economic instability. But more to the point, it will arise as the continuation of the cosmic war between God and the Satan. As we saw in Part 2, the Satan's main instrument of warfare is lies about God, and it was through the church-empire that he did the most damage. And although the church received a deadly wound during the political revolutions of the 18th century, John prophesied that "his fatal wound [would be] healed" (Revelation 13:3). Let's pick up the story from there, in Revelation 13:1–15, focusing on the "other beast" character. What picture of this character does John paint?

___

___

Description of the Other Beast

Notice how the "other beast" arises out of the earth (a terrestrial power), has the characteristics of a lamb (peace, gentleness, Christ), two horns (two governments), no crowns (no kings), and speaks as a dragon (empire / the Satan). It has all the authority of the first beast (worldwide), performs miracles (religious), and deceives the whole world (propaganda) while using its power to force humanity to worship the first beast (the church-empire). Those who resist will be charged with a civil offense and face imprisonment, even death. All of this, John says, is enforced by the "other beast."

But who is this other beast? John never spells it out. As usual, we must allow the prophecy to walk hand in hand with history. The vision points us beyond the time when the church-empire's fatal wound took place. During this time, John sees that a nation would arise, have Christian attributes, two governing principles with no king, worldwide power, and be intimately connected to religious themes and the first beast, which is the church-empire.

History points us in only one direction: *The United States of America*. In 1798, when the historic church received its deadly wound, the USA was becoming a powerful nation. Because many of the colonizers were Christian, they established a government based on Christian principles, including freedom of religion and democracy (two horns, no king). However, despite the nation's enlightened ideals, the vision reveals that it was—in its inmost being—yet another weapon in the Satan's arsenal to oppress, deceive, and war against God.

The lamb-like nature of America, along with its dragon speech, can be clearly seen throughout its history. From its cruel conquest and colonization of the indigenous nations to its economic dependence on the human trafficking / slave market of its formative years, followed by Jim Crow; red-lining; gentrification; and mass-incarceration, it is clear that this government, regardless of its rich Christian heritage, was ultimately no different to Babylon, Greece, Medo-Persia, Rome, or the church-empire. Like all regimes before it, it rose to the zenith of power through the exploitation of the voiceless.

Therefore, the question "how could this possibly happen?" is not a difficult one to answer. No human kingdom will ever be righteous. It's just not possible. Even the great nation of America, dedicated to the principle of freedom, speaks as a dragon. The Satan's war against God has not yet ended. His beast received a deadly political wound, and if he wants to regain the power he once had, he will need the allegiance of the most powerful nation on earth. It's only logical that, in some deceptive way, the rebel will secure a renewed religio-political alliance between the US and the church-empire in order to launch his final campaign against God.

How Can We Embody this Radical Love in the Midst of Chaos?

However, the prophetic vision doesn't revolve around a mere pessimistic foreshadowing of human society. Nested within the vision, there is this grand hope toward which everything points. There is a new society coming, populated by a new humanity recreated in the image of the new human—Jesus. But this new thing is not merely future tense; it is a present reality. The vision points to a spiritual underground, a people who—while far from perfect—are filled with a radical, supernatural love. Love for this community is much more than ideological or philosophical ideas, but rather, an embodied, corporeal pattern lived out in tangible, real-time humanity.

This new humanity emerges in tension with a society operating in full self-preservation mode. They are lied about, betrayed, imprisoned and killed, but, just like their ancestor Jesus, they go on loving. A grand metamorphosis has taken place. No longer slaves to the matrix of self, they demonstrate the beauty of a humanity that dances harmoniously with the tempos of divine love.

But how can we embody this radical love in our own lives and be a part of this spiritual underground? There is only one answer: *Jesus*. When we mediate on him, center our lives and thoughts in him, love on him, spend time with him, and allow him to heal our wounds and scars—to pour his love in us and through us—we grow into our new identity and our new attachment in him.

Here are three simple rhythms you can nurture in your life, each day, to celebrate this transformational connection with Jesus. Explore the accompanying texts with your fellow travelers.

1.

Realize that you don't have to manufacture or replicate the new humanity of Jesus. The truth is that Jesus has already perfected it with his own life, death, and resurrection. The first step into this new humanity, then, is not to try and copy or replicate Jesus but to enter into a reciprocal connection with him. When you do, his new humanity begins to flow organically through you (John 15:5).

2.

Because Jesus has already perfected this new, love-centered humanity, his new identity is also now yours by faith. You might feel like the old human you once were, but Jesus promises that he has already given you a new identity. Refuse to define yourself according to the old attachments and, instead, choose to live out of your new identity, completely fulfilled in him. A practical way to do this is to commit your time and resources to serving the suffering and hurting in our world, to use your voice and influence for the disenfranchised—to active humanitarian service in your own city/town (2 Corinthians 5:17, Romans 6:11).

3.

Another great way to live out your new identity in Jesus is to start each day by asking Jesus to live out his new humanity in you, especially in the spaces where your old self wants to take control. Practice this divine-human synchronicity each day, inviting Jesus into deeper relationship and allowing him to manifest his perfect love in your relationships with others (Galatians 2:20).

HEALING TEACHING

Many fundamentalist religious communities today place an unhealthy focus on the apocalyptic themes of the Bible. Conspiracy theories, cynical dystopian visions of the future, fear mongering, the demonization of others, and a sectarian "only we know the truth" attitude tends to define these groups. To make matters more difficult, these ideas often align with far-right conservative politics that only amplifies the us-vs-them mentality. However, the apocalyptic vision of scripture is not intended to be weaponized for harm but to give humanity hope in the midst of injustice and oppression. When read with Jesus at the centre, these visions are a healing reminder to the suffering and marginalized that the pain fueled by systems of power will not last forever. A day of liberation and a reconstructed neighbourhood of relational oneness is on its way.

REFLECT

The Satan's war against God is not over. While we live in an age of prosperity, the Bible prophesies a coming social catastrophe and the resurgence of religious oppression. The deadly wound is being healed, and soon the first beast, the second beast, and the dragon will unite to war against God and his church. But his church is composed of those who have fallen in love with Jesus and who have been reborn from the old fallen humanity into Christ's new redeemed humanity. As they, daily, bathe in his love, their hearts are molded by the Holy Spirit to love like he does. And when society collapses, Jesus depicts them as enduring in love in the midst of injustice and absurdity. This supernatural expression of agape love will continue until the gospel has reached all nations and Jesus returns to establish a new kingdom ruled by eternal love.

CONNECT

Review _____

Open _____

Ask _____

Decide _____

ENGAGE

Scan the QR code to watch this chapter's accompanying Reflection video.

SCAN ME: THE COLLAPSE

3. THE MARK

In the last chapter, we explored John's vision in Revelation 13. We saw that a portion of this vision parallels the visions of Daniel and has already been fulfilled. However, the second portion remains in the future. While Daniel's visions lead us to the moment that the church-empire received a deadly, political wound, John takes us to a time when the wound will be healed.

The first beast (church-empire) appears to regain its power with the help of the second beast (the United States), in the same way in which it first gained its power from the dragon (Rome). John then says that the second beast will use its power (civic, systemic, military) to force the world (global alliances) to worship the first beast (a new age of religio-political oppression).

This narrative is but the continuation of the war of the two kingdoms: the empire of mankind—self-centered and corrupt—in conflict with the principles of love and justice, the cornerstones of the kingdom of heaven.

However, there is more to this story. It's found in Revelation 13:16–18. Read the text and summarize below. Take some time to discuss the mark of the beast. What do you think it represents?

_____
_____
_____

The mark of the beast is a topic that has given rise to countless interpretations, ranging from the interesting to the ridiculous (with a few comical ones in between). However, in order to identify what the mark is, we must stay within the narrative of scripture. Therefore, let's go back to Revelation 13:11–18 and work our way down the events that John lays out for us. Read the verses in your Bible and then come back for a breakdown of the story the vision is telling.

I.

The second beast (USA) has global power, and gives its power and allegiance over to the first beast (church-empire). The deadly wound is now completely healed, making the church-empire capable of, once again, pursuing its counter-narrative agenda.

2.

The second beast is able to perform miracles and use them to deceive the masses into believing it is aligned with God. It then mimics the intolerance of the first beast, by forcing the people to worship the first beast. This will be a time of religious oppression.

3.

Apart from the threat of death, the beasts employ a type of economic intolerance. Those who do not have the mark of the beast on their right hand (symbolizing deeds) or on their forehead (symbolizing allegiance) are not able to buy or sell. All who wish to remain faithful to God during this time will be completely shut out.

4.

The name of the first beast is not given; though all the historical clues lead us back toward the church-empire. However, this is bigger than the church-empire as well. The prophetic themes of a mark, name, or number of the beast represent humanity's collective rebellion against God. In scripture, a name is symbolic of character, and the number seven represents perfection in love. The beast's name, amounting to 666, speaks of a character that may appear close to godly but is bereft of love. In many ways, the final conflict being depicted here envisions a coalition of all empires, religions, and systems at war with the kingdom of Jesus.

So, here is what we know. The first and second beast unite, and, in doing so, the Satan's counter-narrative agenda spreads through the world. Unlike the Dark Ages, the rise of globalization, social media, and AI makes it possible for this counter-narrative to engulf our collective human consciousness. The character of this first beast is one of rebellion against God, while appearing to be his ally. The masses will be conned by this religio-political alliance. Many others will openly welcome its totalitarian regime. But there will be those who oppose it in favor of "a better country...whose architect and builder is God" (Hebrews 11:16, 10). This tribe will become the object of the accuser's wrath.

But what about the mark of the beast? Is it a digital chip? A vaccine? An identification number? The Bible never gives us a tangible picture. However, it gives us enough clues so that we can construct a meaningful understanding, to help us confront the mark when it emerges.

Read Ezekiel 9:3–4, Deuteronomy 6:8, John 16:13, Ezekiel 20:12, Exodus 20:8–11, Revelation 7:2–3, and Revelation 22:4! Contrast these with Revelation 4:11 and Matthew 25:41. What do we gather from these texts?

_____
_____
_____

THE MARK OF THE BEAST

- *Result of Rebellion*
- *Identifies the Loyal*
- *Intolerance, Man-centered*
- *Allegiance to Man*
- *Religio-Political, Earthly Power*
- *Results in Death*

THE SEAL OF GOD

- *Result of the Gospel*
- *Identifies the Loyal*
- *Love, God-centered*
- *Allegiance to Jesus*
- *Kingdom of Heaven*
- *Results in Eternal Life*

Whatever the mark of the beast is, it is in direct contrast to God's seal. But before we tie this all together, lets look at two more biblical themes that are connected to the seal of God.

THE SABBATH

- *A sign of social justice and equity (Exodus 31:13)*
- *A sign of being in rhythm with God's heart of love (Exodus 31:17)*
- *A sign of God's new humanity (Ezekiel 20:12)*

THE HOLY SPIRIT

- *A sign of oneness with God (2 Corinthians 1:21–22)*
- *A sign of being in rhythm with God's heart of love (Ephesians 1:12–14)*
- *A sign of God's new humanity (Ephesians 4:30)*

Shabbat (Rest)

Throughout scripture, the Sabbath is repeatedly referred to as a "sign" that identifies who God's people are. This is because the Sabbath represents all the diverse facets of God's character and government. The Sabbath equalizes humanity in a world of racism, sexism, and nationalism. The Sabbath resists the exploitation of nature in a world dominated by the corporate bottom line. The Sabbath celebrates the inherent value of all creation by resisting our exploitation, commodification, and objectification. The Sabbath celebrates God's posture toward us, as the gift giver, and man, as the gift receiver. And finally, it celebrates his finished work of creation, salvation, and cosmic restoration.

Is it no wonder then that the Sabbath has been lost sight of in modern Christianity? Throughout its history, the influence of philosophical counter-narratives, anti-antisemitism, religio-political power moves, and a colonized, capitalist reinterpretation of God has led Christian institutions to either forget or openly reject Shabbat as an integral rhythm that belongs to humanity and remains relevant throughout time. In fact, as we saw in the visions of Daniel, the erasure of Shabbat wasn't an accidental thing. The church-empire, as a sign of its authority over all things, including scripture, legislated the change and enforced it with legal power.

When we recognize the Sabbath as a sign of God's character and government that resists the substrates of human dynasty and corporation, it is not surprising that one of history's greatest empires put forth the effort to re-author it, in a way that celebrates its own lust for power.

The Spirit

The Holy Spirit also features as a sign between God and his people. Through the Holy Spirit, we are fused to divinity. His presence in us is what moves us from the original, fallen humanity into the new, restored humanity of Jesus. Oneness with God is restored, our lives enter into harmony with the rhythms of God's loving heart, and our minds are transformed into the very image of Jesus. The Holy Spirit within is, therefore, another sign that identifies God's people. And to make things more intense, the Holy Spirit is explicitly referred to as the one that "seals us" for the day of redemption.

With this in mind, we can see that the seal of God identifies his people, his new society, as those driven by the rhythms of love, whose lives manifest compassion for the suffering, resistance of injustice and empire, and authentic oneness with God himself.

By way of contrast, whatever the mark of the beast will be, it will play a similar roll of identifying those whose lives, postures, and patterns have become synonymous with the interests of power, wealth, and convenience. So what the tangible mark will be is less important than what the mark itself represents—allegiance to the beastly impulse of self upon which all human empires, religions, and corporations are ultimately constructed.

The mark and the seal are ultimately just another way of describing the war between two kingdoms: love and selfishness, relationship and control, truth and lies, freedom and tyranny, the second Adam and the first Adam, fallen humanity and the new humanity. The question we all have to wrestle with then, isn't what tangible (if any) manifestation the mark will have but, rather, which mark (God's or beast's) are my life's patterns and priorities aligned with?

Why Does this Question Matter?

Before we wrap up this vision, lets take a closer look at one of its most radical revelations. We will zoom in on the DNA of this dual-beast, and what it reveals is mind blowing:

THE DUAL-BEAST

- *Two horns like a lamb (Christlike)*
- *Speaks like a dragon (empire)*
- *Exercises authority of first beast (religio-political)*
- *Performs supernatural signs (miraculous)*
- *Legislates worship (religio-political)*
- *Coerces conscience (political oppression)*
- *Its given power (spiritual force behind it)*
- *Punishes through commerce (economic oppression)*

Notice what is at the core of this power's DNA—over and over again we see links and references to church and state. The beast is lamb-like, has religious commitments, performs miracles, legislates worship, and uses civil power to enforce its moral ideals. This abuse of political power is how the system speaks—through laws enacted in the spirit of coercion and control, the very nature of the Satan and his government.

And here is why this is so important: The vision of Revelation 13 shows us that the final power to war against God and his people is not a secular power, an atheist power, or a pagan/non-Christian power. As corrupt and unjust as each of these systems might be in themselves, the vision doesn't focus on them. Instead, Revelations scope is on Christianity and its resurgence as an empire near the end of time. Christian nationalist movements, then, and not secular institutions or leaders, are the main antagonist in the visions of John. In the name of faithfulness and allegiance to God, Christianity once again reaches for the arm of political power and becomes, in itself, an enemy of Creator, pretending to be his friend.

Read 1 Corinthians 13. What does it say about the heart of God? How does this revelation relate to the topic of Christian nationalism and church-empire? And finally, what do you think it would look like for us to live out this kind of love in the here and now?

HEALING TEACHING

The Mark of the Beast is a favourite topic for conspiracy peddlers and toxic theological influencers. For any recovering from the effects of apocalyptic trauma, the entire topic can be unsettling even when viewed from a healthy angle. This is a great place to remember that trauma can be worked through with the proper therapist so that the nervous system can be set free from the pain of the past. It's also helpful to see that themes like the mark of the beast are not in scripture to frighten us but to protest systemic and institutional oppression. When seen from that lens, the topic becomes a song of liberation rather than a vision of gloom.

REFLECT

As the events in Revelation 13 begin to unfold, the world will see a resurgence of religious intolerance, rivaled only by the injustices of the Dark Ages. The other horn will rise up once more to dominate, control, and enforce its agenda on the world. Those who resist will be persecuted. The beast-system, with its counter-narrative and alternative system of salvation and governance, will engulf the world. But the visions of Revelation foresee a spiritual underground who resist the mark because their hearts are sealed by love, a passion for true justice, and complete, unbending allegiance to the way of Jesus.

CONNECT

Review _____
_____

Open _____
_____

Ask _____
_____

Decide _____
_____

ENGAGE

Scan the QR code to watch this chapter's accompanying Reflection video.

SCAN ME: THE MARK

4. THE WARNINGS

The final phase of scripture's narrative is now unfolding, and we are shown a glimpse of a coming age marked by religious intolerance and oppression. The first beast, utilizing the power of the second beast, introduces a religio-political order that demands total allegiance. Religion is forced with the threat of capital and economic punishment. During this time, the underground church—due to its alignment to God's kingdom above human empire—becomes the enemy of the state and is confronted with a fanatical and bigoted society that approves of its persecution.

As these scenes are unfolding, John sees another vision in which three angels descend from the heavens to deliver messages to the people of Earth. Read and comment on Revelation 14:6–13.

FIRST ANGEL

Fear God
Worship Him
Hour of Judgment

SECOND ANGEL

Babylon is Fallen

THIRD ANGEL

Mark of the Beast
God's Wrath
Eternal Destruction

FIRST ANGEL

Share your thoughts on the words of the first angel below. What ideas or pictures come to mind as you read them?

_____
_____
_____

The first angel's message is remarkable. Set against the backdrop of the beast's violent regime, the angel declares the good news of salvation through Jesus—only. This is the narrative that has been woven through every theme we have studied together. We cannot save ourselves, and God has never asked us to. *His salvation is a free gift.* This free gift reflects his character of love and its purpose is to bring us back into relationship with himself. When we receive his salvation, we enter into a new humanity. The ultimate goal of this process is for a "sanctuary God" who loves to "dwell with us" (Exodus 25:8) to be reconnected with us forever. And the way to this relationship is the gift he offers in Jesus. He is not interested in our religious credentials—he is interested in us.

The angel also calls humanity to fear (as in "be in awe of") God, not the beast. The fear of God is the only thing that can set us free from the fear of human empire. When we see how incredible and safe he is, it fills us with immovable confidence. Like the bully in the schoolyard who is no longer scary when the bigger kid promises to protect you, the beast is no longer frightening when our trust is in a God who is greater than all the threats of empire combined.

Finally, the angel reminds humanity to worship God alone because the judgment has already begun. Recall from our studies in Daniel that a final judgment will begin before Jesus returns. In this text, we see that that final cleansing of cosmos is already in motion. In this judgment, Creator defends and celebrates his people. Daniel tells us that, when it ends, the beast will be destroyed and the kingdom will be handed over to God's people. In light of this, the first angel warns everyone not to worship the beast. His destruction is imminent, regardless of how powerful he may appear.

SECOND ANGEL

The second angel's words get a little stranger. He uses lots of symbolism and metaphors. Think of the way in which the narrative has unfolded so far, from Part 1 of this series through to this final phase.

What do you see being communicated in the angel's words?

_____
_____
_____

The second angel's message announces that "Babylon is fallen." A similar message appears in Isaiah 21:9, preceded by God's verdict, "I will bring to an end all the groaning she caused" (2). Babylon, a symbol of the magnificence of human empire, exhibited the same intolerance that the beast exhibits at the end of time. This makes Babylon a symbol of false narratives, an autocracy that thrives on propaganda and injustice. It represents all false institutions, insatiable corporations, and loveless religions. And according to the angel, the day is soon coming when Babylon, as a principle of governance, will be judged and condemned. Later in Revelation, John describes its ultimate collapse this way:

I saw another angel coming down out of the sky...He cried with a mighty voice, saying, "Fallen, fallen is Babylon the great...she will be utterly burned with fire; for the Lord God who has judged her is strong..." Thus with violence will Babylon, the great city, be thrown down, and will be found no more at all. —Revelation 18: 1–2, 8, 21 (NASB)

THIRD ANGEL

The final angel now enters the scene. Like the first two above, take some time to mediate and decipher his words. Then share your ideas below.

_____
_____
_____

The third angel brings it all together. Notice that it says, "Anyone who worships the beast and his [image]...must drink the wine of God's anger" (v9).

The religio-political order of the first and second beast are clearly a part of Babylon. The church-empire and all who ally themselves with it in the end of time fall under the symbol of Babylon, as institutions and systems that convey lies about God and perpetuate suffering, inequality, and injustice on the earth. And because all falsehood, counter-narratives, and idolatry are about to be destroyed, the angel warns that anyone who remains aligned to this religio-political empire, worships it, and receives it's identifying mark will suffer the same fate.

For this reason, in Revelation 18, an invitation is given from heaven: "come out of her (Babylon) my people, that you have no participation in her sins, and that you don't receive of her plagues" (Revelation 18:4). The sins of Babylon are the sins of empire: the extortion of the earth, the abuse of the poor, the oppression of the voiceless, and the coercion of the state. In the name of economic and national security, empire justifies craft, trickery, and assassination and protects the elite and wealthy at the expense of its citizens, migrants, and refugees. Even at its best, empire cannot help but perpetuate inequity and suffering. So God, in judgment long overdue, will bring it to a complete and irreversible end.

Read Revelation 14:12. What does this verse mean to you in light of the rest of the overall story we have been exploring?

_____
_____
_____

Three primary themes emerge in this text: The patience of the saints, the commandments of God, and the faith of Jesus. These three themes, when viewed in context with the story being told, paint a remarkable contrast. As the bigotry and intolerance of human empire reaches the apex of rebellion, John depicts an underground society of people who are living to a totally different rhythm. That rhythm is one of calmness in the midst of social exasperation, harmony with God's law of love in the midst of global allegiance to the law of national interest, and complete trust in the faith of Jesus in the midst of a culture that has placed its trust in the beastly power of a church-state alliance.

This final phrase, "faith of Jesus," is key to our entire understanding of this alternative community. Their faith is rooted and centered, not in any faith inherent or active within themselves but in the faith "of" Jesus. In other words, the members of this community are defined by their confidence in the faithfulness of Jesus, not by a focus on their own faith-efforts. It is by centering their thoughts and contemplation on the unfailing, unbending faithfulness of their king, Jesus, that they are able to transcend the chaos of universal collapse and live with serenity and love in the midst of a society that persecutes them. Because they know, despite their failures and doubts and the indescribable pandemonium that surrounds them, that Jesus is faithful and, even when it seems like chaos has won, he will keep the promise he has made—the promise of a new humanity, a new society, a new kingdom, a new heaven, and a new earth where justice reigns.

HEALING TEACHING

Sectarian churches believe things like, "we alone know the truth," or "we alone are right." In this view, every other church, faith-tribe, and denomination is evil, demonic, and Babylon. However, the Babylon vision is there to show us that Babylon is a coercive and arrogant system and to warn us to leave that system and its rhythms behind. This means abandoning our own impulses of control, our own sense of self-importance, and our own coercive and unhealthy dogmas. We don't leave Babylon by merely leaving a church we think is bad. We leave it by surrendering our impulse of control to Jesus and allowing his relational heart to flow through us and out to others.

REFLECT

The three angel's messages warn us to keep our faith in Jesus and live for him alone. We are now living on the cusp of the first angel's message. Our task is to share the good news of Jesus, call people to abandon Babylon and its oppressive systems, and proclaim the reality of a present-time, cosmic judgment. Jesus is returning, and when he does, every unjust empire that dwells on the earth will meet its final hour.

CONNECT

Review _____
_____

Open _____
_____

Ask _____
_____

Decide _____
_____

ENGAGE

Scan the QR code to watch this chapter's accompanying Reflection video.

SCAN ME: THE WARNING

5. THE RETURN

One of the trickiest parts of navigating Revelation's visions is the very real presence of apocalyptic trauma. For many today, cynical, end-of-the-world rhetoric, dystopian narratives, guilt-driven activism, and the endless round of conspiracy theories have left an ugly scar in the psyche. When reading the visions of John, then, the scar can feel like its about to get torn open again.

While religious trauma is a real experience that may necessitate professional counseling, there is a simple approach to navigate John's message in a way that nurtures healing and hope rather than despair and fear. That approach is simple: when reading Revelation, we must read the visions from the bottom up.

By "bottom," we mean from the perspective of the suffering, oppressed, and marginalized in the world. When read through their eyes, the visions become songs of liberation and hope rather than despair. This bottom-up approach is exactly what is needed as we enter into the final chapters of Revelation; in which God dismantles man's empire in preparation for a new kingdom.

Turn to Revelation 18 and 19. What picture do you see being painted in these chapters?

_____

_____

_____

SINS OF EMPIRE

- Political Corruption
- Violation of Human Rights
- Economic Indulgence
- Abuse of Power
- Resource Control
- Environmental Crime
- Human Trafficking and Slavery
- Murder of the Innocent

FALL OF EMPIRE

- Torment and Sorrow
- Death and Famine
- Incinerated with Fire
- Economic Collapse
- Abandonment
- Irreversible Destruction
- Thrown into a Lake of Fire with its Allies

NEW SOCIETY

- Leave Babylon
- Rejoice at its Destruction
- Worship God
- Wedding Feast
- Adorned in Justice
- Centered on Jesus, its king

In painful and agonizing detail, Revelation 18 describes the gruesome sins of human-empire. But it also describes the verdict of the cosmic judgment that has taken place—a judgment that has not only laid its opportunistic scandals bare but that has also determined its fate. Empire is deconstructed—its power, luxury, and privilege turned inside out—and its legacy and identity cast into divine fire to be removed forever.

But that's not the end of the story. Human empire has finally met its end, but humanity has not. A new humanity whose life and love flow from the second Adam, Jesus himself, is now brought to the center and given possession of the earth. This new humanity celebrates the demise of the old order of things and establishes a society and civilization that reflects the image of Jesus. This is a kingdom adorned in justice and compassion—a new world where a new story will be written. With the legacy of fallen empire ground to powder, this new humanity enters into a new chapter of the human experience, in which tales, adventures, and memories will emerge that bear, not the imprint of injustice and suffering but of peace and siblinghood—a global village defined by love.

But we are getting ahead of ourselves. Before this new society begins, Jesus must first return to the earth to judge empire and rescue his community.

Read and discuss Revelation 6:12–14; 16:20–21; and Luke 21:25–28. What picture do these verses paint?

_____
_____
_____

The depth of this narrative cannot be overemphasized. In Jesus's day, a marriage went through three stages: first, the arrangement; second, the "betrothal"; third, was the marriage itself.

When a betrothal was made, the two parties shared a cup of wine together before both families. Then, the husband-to-be would go back to his father's house and build a partition in it for him and his wife to live in. After a year, the husband would complete the addition and then return, with an entourage of friends and family, to pick up his bride. Together, they would parade back with both their families and friends to the husband's house. The wedding feast would then take place, followed by the consummation of the marriage.

Read the following texts and discuss how they relate to this ancient Hebrew practice and the second coming of Jesus: John 14:2–3 and Matthew 26:26–29.

_____

_____

_____

The second coming of Jesus is a romantic story of a sanctuary God wanting to dwell with his people. But it is also about a judge coming to bring an utter end to all injustice. Every political party, ideology, and philosophy will be erased. Every national legacy will become meaningless. Every governmental structure will collapse. Likewise, all religion will be exposed for its bankruptcy. Every lie about God will be vindicated. Every system that monetizes guilt, exploits the spiritually hungry, and defrauds the hearts of men will crumble. And best of all, every social ill will be healed. No more broken families, loneliness, bullying, suffering, crime, indifference, betrayal, or pain. These things will pass away for good.

The earth now lays desolate. The redeemed have been taken; the enemies of love have met their fate. According to John, the saved erupt into song. Like the children of Israel, who sang and danced after their deliverance from Egypt, God's people celebrate their rescue from Babylon.

We are now approaching the final act in the narrative of scripture. The age of empire and protest has ended. With the return of Jesus, the story is ushered into its final stage. The "New Creation" is about to begin.

REFLECT

The Bible says that when Jesus returns, those who have loved him will be "caught up...in the clouds to meet the Lord in the air, and so we will be with the Lord forever" (1 Thessalonians 4:17). Pay special attention to the four letter word "with." This will be the greatest moment in the history of the world and of your life. You will see Jesus face to face. A new chapter and a new dimension of experience now unfolds before you. But the best part is this: Love won. Jesus overcame. Eternal "withness" has been restored.

CONNECT

Review _____
_____

Open _____
_____

Ask _____
_____

Decide _____
_____

ENGAGE

Scan the QR code to watch this chapter's accompanying Reflection video.

SCAN ME: THE RETURN

6. THE MILLENNIUM

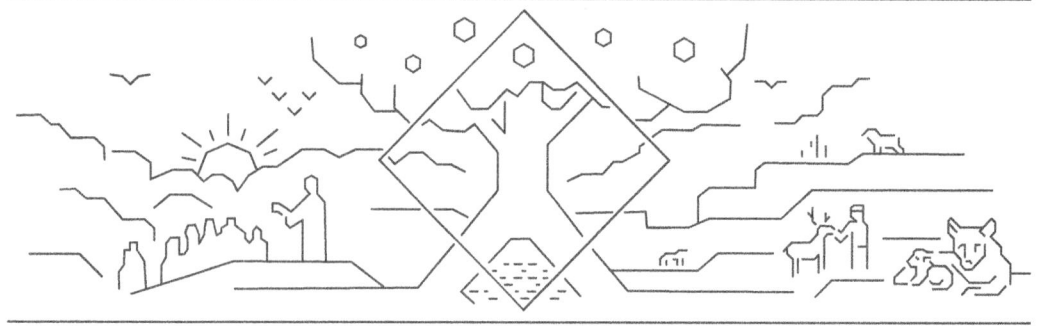

Revelation is an uncomfortable book. Its vision of a coming social collapse is far from romantic and optimistic. And even though its foreshadowing has not yet come to pass, the images of this coming dystopian age help us discern that, even now, the machinations of empire are slowly working toward this grand, final onslaught that will bring about an age of unprecedented chaos and injustice.

However, this stark before and after is only the reality for a privileged few in the world today. For most of humanity, chaos, loss and catastrophe are daily realities that they long to be delivered from. And herein lies the beauty of Revelation; despite the chaos it envisions, John sees a trans-terrestrial and upside-down kingdom—one which operates entirely on the ethic of other-centered love—break through the perimeter of the earth and depose every oppressive institution and beastly government. The stone of Daniel 2 (return of Jesus) collides with and crushes human empire.

However, the return of Jesus is not the end. Instead, the visions launch us into a dramatic epilogue. Revelation 20:1–3 introduces this end-plot with these words:

Then I saw an angel coming down from heaven, holding the key of the abyss and a great chain in his hand. And he laid hold of the dragon, the serpent of old, who is the devil and the Satan, and bound him for a thousand years; and he threw him into the abyss, and shut it and sealed it over him, so that he would not deceive the nations any longer…(NASB)

abyssos

Abyssos is the Greek word used in this verse to describe the place to which the arch-rebel is bound after the return of Jesus. It is the same Greek word used to describe the state of the earth in Genesis 1:2, when it says, "The earth was formless and void…" In other words, after the second coming, the earth will go back to being an abyss. It is in this sense that Lucifer will be bound with no one to lure or manipulate. And during this period of time the story says that the redeemed will reign with God for a thousand years.

Read Revelation 20:4. What do you think this text means?

_____

_____

_____

John sees a partnership between those who have been given authority to judge and those who have suffered death at the hands of empire. These victims of political and religious violence are raised to reign with Christ and participate in the final phase of cosmic judgment. And while the text never explains why God does this, there are three reasonable possibilities. First, the millennium allows the redeemed time to process and heal from the trauma of oppression. Second, the time frame provides the saved with a chance to review everything God has done and answer any lingering questions about his fairness. Finally, the millennium psychologically prepares us for what happens next:

To see what this is, read the following texts in the order shown: Revelation 20:7–8, 21: 2, 20:11–13, 15 and 9.

_____

_____

_____

When the millennium ends, Jesus will return to Earth for a third time, and the lost will be raised to face their final judgment. During this time, each person will stand before God as though there were no other. The divine tribunal of social/cosmic justice enters its final phase. No stone has been left unturned.

When the scene ends, John explains the final act of God's judgment: fire and destruction. The wicked are completely and utterly annihilated—body and soul—never to rise again.

Turn now to verses 10 and 14–15 of Revelation 20.
How does God's judgment on sin end?

_____

_____

_____

In order to understand this closing scene, we need to go back to the sanctuary. Recall that the sanctuary is one of the central themes in the entire Bible. It reveals the gospel in symbols and metaphors that basically boil down to one thing: *God wants to be with us*. This state of "withness" is not a mere idea but a reality God is continually pursuing. It places he and us in the same time and place. This key is one that unlocks the character of God in amazing ways. He is not a god sitting in a faraway realm, comfortably removed from our suffering and pain. Rather, he "sanctuaries" with us.

The sanctuary narrative is a revelation of this. The lamb, which represents Jesus, is the answer to our divine-human separation. In his life, death, and resurrection a reintegration of humanity and divinity takes place. However, its obvious that even after Jesus accomplished his mission, sin and empire continued—but not for long. God's cosmic judgment, which begins before Christ's return, is the death knell that brings about the complete eradication of sin. This final eradication is pictured in the a strange act of the sanctuary that Leviticus refers to as "the goat for Azazel."

Read about it in Leviticus 16:5–26 and then turn to the chart below (larger, user friendly version in the next page) for a summary.

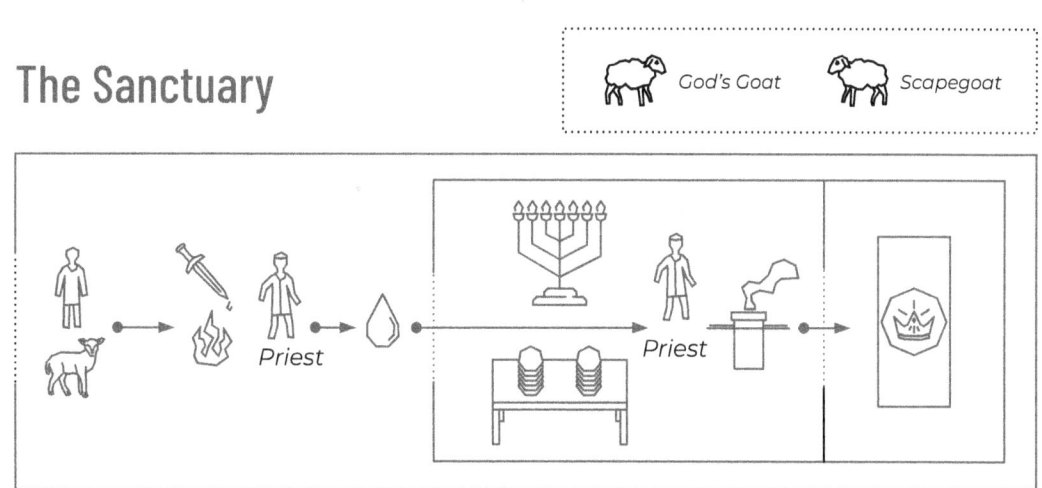

Before we explore what the goat for Azazel—or "scapegoat"—means, let's take a final review through the symbols in the sanctuary.

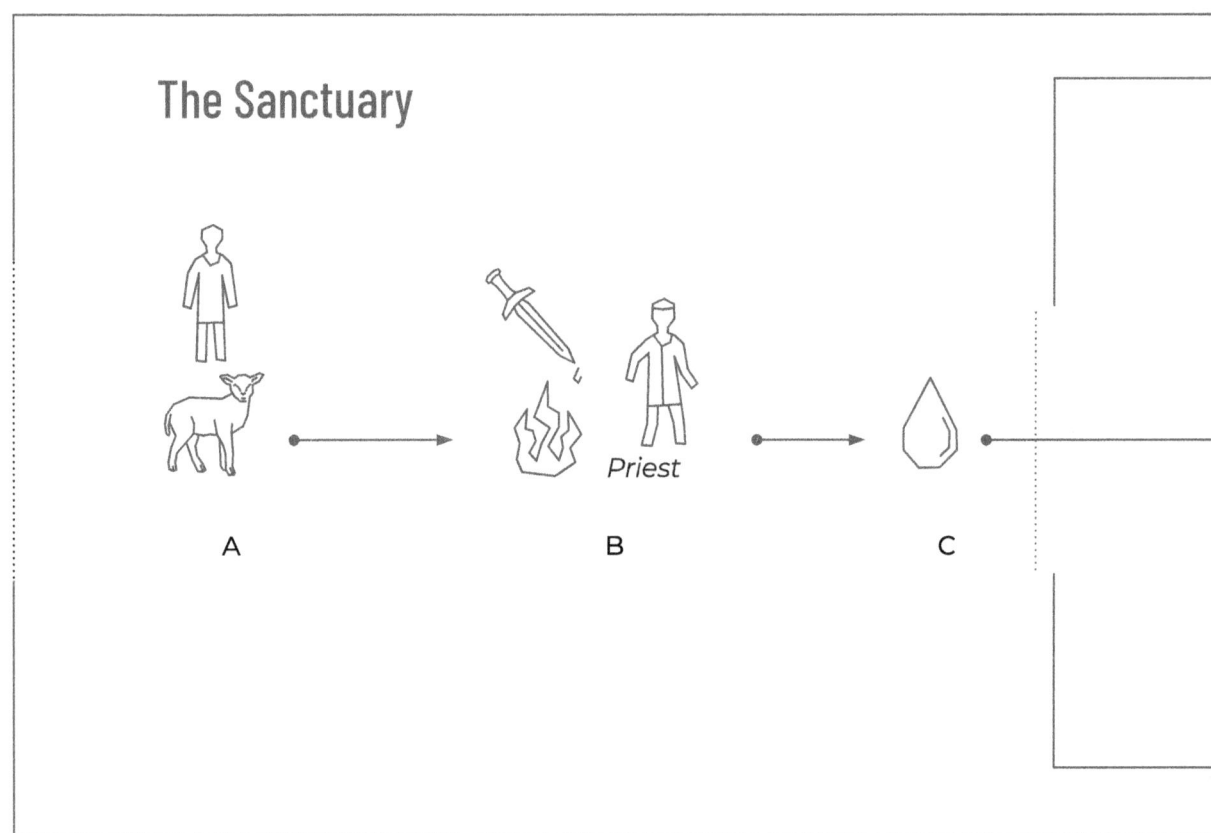

A Person brings lamb into sanctuary.
Lamb represents Jesus, who restores us to oneness with God.

B Priest kills lamb and takes blood inside.
Jesus absorbed our separation, and his life stands in our place.

C Priest washes himself before entering the tent.
Jesus is our spotless priest.

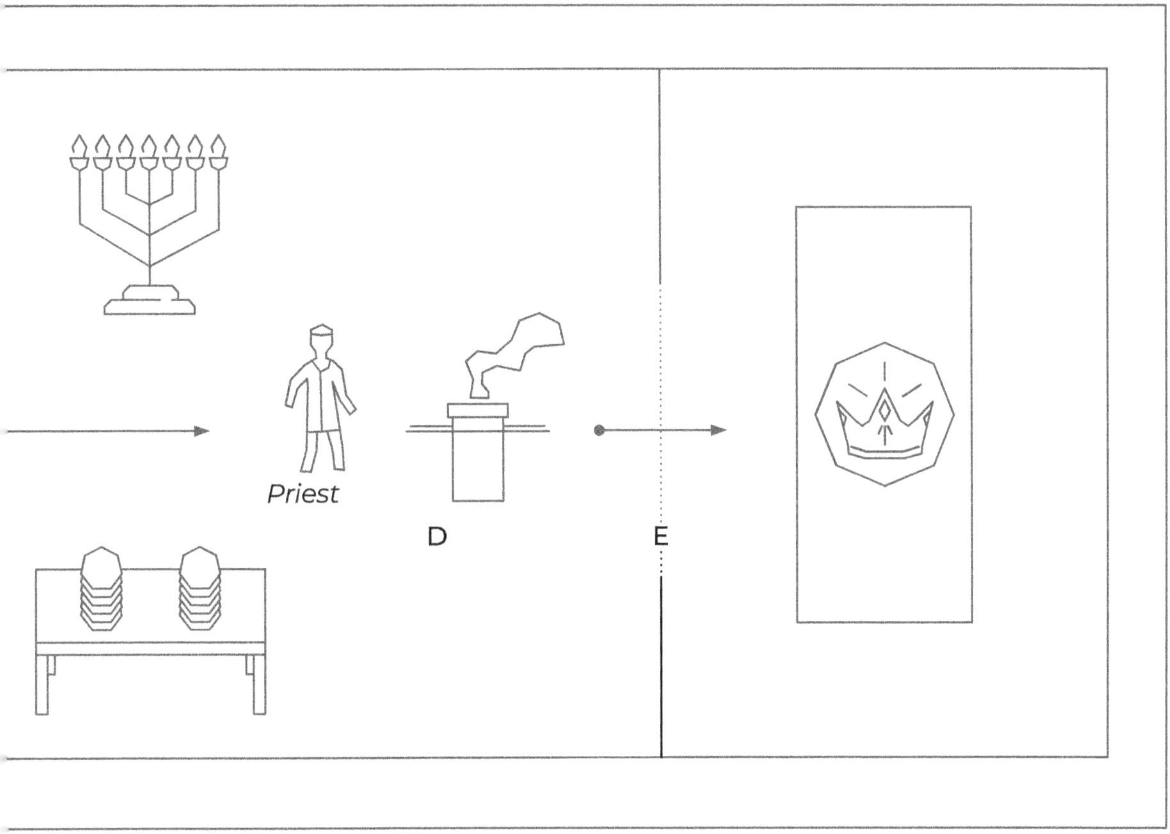

D Priest presents blood before the veil.
Jesus applies his sacrifice and new humanity to his people.

E Once a year, Priest goes behind the veil.
Once in time, Jesus begins the final judgment.

F Once a year, the scapegoat is removed.
The empire of self is forever annihilated.

The sanctuary basically depicts the war between good and evil and how God would restore things back to their original design. The center of the entire narrative is Jesus. He is the solution to our separation from God. When the judgment ends, the separation is forever undone. Sin is eradicated, and God's people dwell with him forever as he originally designed they would. Because the judgment has ended and there is no more need for a sacrifice, the goat for Azazel is not a sacrifice for sins. In fact, it has no salvation function. Once the judgment ends, salvation is complete. So then, what is this goat for?

The text never really explains it. However, this is what we can gather. First, the goat for Azazel, as mentioned above, is not a sacrifice, and it doesn't pardon sin. So, it doesn't appear to represent Jesus. Second, the goat is removed from the people of God. Since the entire sanctuary narrative is about bringing God and his people together again, it once again seems unlikely that this goat, who is forever separated from the community, represents Jesus. Third, once the process of salvation is complete, the scapegoat seems to act as a sort of dumpster. The *NIV Cultural Backgrounds Study Bible* refers to it as a "garbage truck" that "purge[s] the Israelite community."

In other words, sin has been forgiven and removed from the community. But something remains of all of this sin, and this remaining substance is placed on the scapegoat, who is then sent out into the wilderness to die alone.

This metaphor parallels Revelation 20 in remarkable ways. While God's people are in heaven with him participating in the judgment, the arch-nemesis is left alone on the earth with no one to harass for a thousand years. It's as if he is in a wilderness. And as the redeemed pour through the books in heaven, one conclusion leaps forth—God is in no way responsible for sin. Lucifer is the one who is solely responsible.

All of the pain and horror is thus placed on him, and in a final act of judgment and closure he, along with the ideological empire of his making, is held ultimately responsible for all the suffering, injustice, and catastrophe that sin has wrought.

In the end, the Satan is cast into the lake of fire to perish, along with death (separation), the false prophet (lies about God), and the beast (human empire), never to rise again.

HEALING TEACHING

There are theological systems that push the idea that God is beyond questioning. In this view, God is no different to the despotic strong men of fascist and communist regimes. However, the biblical dream of the Millennium shows that while it might be true that a sovereign God doesn't have to explain himself to us, the God of scripture chooses to do so anyway. He is a God of relationship whose main interest is our healing, not his ego. He opens himself and his judgments to mere mortals and welcomes us into the mystery of his rule.

REFLECT

The war between good and evil is over. God's people have dwelled with him in heaven, performing a work of judgment for a thousand years. When that work ends, God's city relocates to the earth, where the judgment against the wicked is executed in full. The Satan—instigator of the cosmic conflict between good and evil—is held ultimately responsible for the sin that has disrupted the harmony of God's universe for so long. He wanders the earth alone and is finally destroyed, bringing a total end to a war that has brought immeasurable suffering to the cosmos.

CONNECT

Review _____
_____

Open _____
_____

Ask _____
_____

Decide _____
_____

ENGAGE

Scan the QR code to watch this chapter's accompanying Reflection video.

SCAN ME: THE MILLENIUM

7. THE MORTALS

Love wins. The war that the Satan has waged from the beginning ends. And we are living on the cusp of this final chapter. With the cosmic judgment already underway, it is only a matter of time before Jesus returns. The Bible then predicts one final battle. The empire of self, led by the meta-rebel, will gather into a climactic horde.

As the millennium ends, legions as numerous as the sand on the seashore surround the city of God (Revelation 20:7–9). This is the Satan's final blitzkrieg. The war machine that follows him, composed of every angel and human who has ever rejected God and the principles of his government of love, is prepared for a final assault. There is no agape love in their hearts. They are now fully in the image of their self-centered king.

The next thing John sees is God sitting on a throne (Revelation 20:11). The books are opened and the verdict against the offenders is pronounced. Then, fire comes down from heaven and consumes them. And it is here that we encounter one of the biggest questions about God's justice and moral character.

There are some who say that this fire will torment the wicked for all eternity and others who say that the fire will simply consume them. The view we embrace has massive implications for the truth of who God is and what he is like. In order to make sense of this, we have to return to the beginning.

In the beginning, God created...(Genesis 1:1)

As we saw in Part 1, God creates out of love. But the question today is this: What kind of reality would a God of love create?

This question may seem strange, but it has direct implications to understanding God's character in light of death and eternal judgment. And thankfully, the Bible answers the question.

The creation story in Genesis quotes God describing his creation as "good" and "very good." Therefore, the reality that God creates is one that is good in every way. Contrast this with other world views to see the difference:

NATURALIST

Physical reality.

No ultimate good.

Physical world is neither good nor bad.

PAGAN

Physical/spiritual reality.

Physical = ultimate good.

Spiritual realm is bad; physical realm is good.

GREEK/EASTERN

Physical/spiritual reality

Spiritual = ultimate good

Spiritual realm is good; physical realm is bad

TRANS-HUMAN

Physical/Bio-tech reality

Bio-tech = Ultimate good

Bio-tech is good; Physical is bad

The chart above describes how some of the most popular worldviews perceive reality. For the atheist, there is no such thing as good. Reality does not go any further than what is natural, and the things that happen in this world are neither good nor bad; they are merely the blind process of evolution. In pagan thought, that which is good is physical. The pursuit of materiality is supreme, and the spiritual world is an undefined (sometimes impersonal, sometimes helpful, often evil) force that must be manipulated for gain in the physical world (via magic, sorcery, incantations, etc.). In Greek/Eastern thought, reality is split into two realms: the spiritual realm is considered good, and the physical realm is considered bad. All humans are spirits trapped in a physical body. The physical body is viewed as a prison we must escape in order to enter the good realm above. This idea is also seen in the Buddhist and Hindu concept of reincarnation. This cycle keeps us trapped in the physical realm and must be escaped.

In the modern age, a new perspective known as "Trans-humanism" has emerged. While built on a naturalist paradigm, the goal of trans-humanism is to blend man with machine in order to enhance our capabilities, take control of the process of evolution, and ultimately achieve immortality, either through the reversal of aging or uploading human consciousness into a digital plane where it can exist forever. In this view, the physical realm has too many limitations (disease, decay, etc.), so the goal is to enhance, or transcend, it through the use of technology. Digital uploading or bio-tech enhancements act as non-religious equivalents of a "spirit" realm that the trans-humanist is aiming to reach.

So, we have before us three options for how reality is organized. Either there is no good in reality, the ultimate good is our physical desires, or the ultimate good is in the spirit (or digital) realm. If this is the case, then the physical and spiritual realms must be separated—one being good and the other bad.

So, here is the key question. If you are this God of intimate love, which of the above realities would you create? Is it the Naturalist, Pagan, Greek/Eastern, or Transhuman? Or is it none of the above? Hopefully your answer was "none of the above." And if it was, then you are in good company. The Bible teaches a completely different view of reality.

In order to comprehend what it is, let's embark on a journey through scripture. First turn to Genesis 2:7. Notice how Moses describes the way in which God created man:

BODY BREATH BEING

According to Genesis, the ultimate good is the heart of God. He creates out of love and declares his creation good day after day. Then, when it's all over he declares it "very good" because all of creation is a reflection of his heart—especially human beings who are made "in his image." Unlike the world views above, God declares both the physical and spiritual "good" and "very good." However, there is something else that sets the Bible apart from all the other views.

The Hebrew word for "living being" is "nephesh," which is commonly translated as "soul." But this soul does not come from some "higher" ether to be trapped within a body as the ancient Greeks thought. Likewise, it does not exist separate from the body. Rather, it is intimately connected to the body. The human being is a holistic combination of body (physical) + breath of life (spiritual). The end result is a living consciousness (being or soul). Almost like a birth, our consciousness begins to exist anew, though the complex developmental process of body and breath in the womb. This view sets the Bible apart from all the other views. While they elevate either the physical or the spiritual above one another, the Bible teaches that these two are not actually separate, but united. Both the physical and the spiritual are interwoven and cannot be split. And together they form the "very good" reality that God brought into being.

Turn to Genesis 3:19. What did God say to Adam after he sinned? Compare it to Ecclesiastes 12:7.

_____
_____
_____

Notice what Solomon says that when we die the dust (body) returns to the earth. However, it doesn't stop there. He goes on to say that the spirit returns to God. But what is the spirit? Is it our consciousness? Or is it God's breath of life?

Take a moment to discuss this, and pay special attention to the phrase "will return to God who gave it" in Genesis 2:7. What is it that God gave?

_____
_____
_____

God did not give us a soul, where a disembodied ghost is taken from its "spirit-realm" and placed inside a body. Rather, God gave us the breath of life, which is his. When God gave that spark to the inanimate body, the result was a new consciousness that had never existed before. This places both soul and body in the category of "good" and "very good."

God created a holistic reality, which explains why he invites us to maintain a healthy body, to treat it as his "temple," as well as a healthy mind. The human being is a combination of two gifts: a body, which we did not make and a breath of life, which comes only from God. When these two fuse together, the result is an entirely new, radically unique, magical phenomenon that has never been seen before in all reality: *You.*

Ghosts, Spirits, and the Afterlife

One of the implications of this biblical view is that it fundamentally alters the way we think of ghosts. In most other spiritual worldviews, a portal is left open between our physical dimension and a spectral dimension, in which the actively-conscious spirits of our loved ones reside. With this portal open, it is then assumed that the spirits of our deceased loved ones can still impact history, by transferring information, providing guidance and wisdom, and communicating content to those of us who still occupy the realm of the living.

However, if the Bible is correct in teaching that the dead are in an inactive, unconscious state then this means our dead loved ones cannot possibly communicate with us from beyond the grave. But this forces a very uncomfortable question: What do we do with ghosts?

Take a tour through the following verses to see what you discover:

| *Job 14:10–12* | *Ecclesiastes 9:5* | *2 Kings 21:6* |
| *Psalm 146:3–4* | *Leviticus 19:31* | *Isaiah 8:19* |

Occult teachings and practices maintain an open portal between the realm of the living and the realm of the dead. But if the dead are in a state of "consciousness suspension" until judgment day, then any spirit we speak to who purports to be the active consciousness of our dead loved ones must necessarily be a lying spirit. And to be placed under the influence of a lying spirit is both spiritually and existentially dangerous. Scripture's view serves as a warning to protect us from coming under the influence of this corrupt cosmic intelligence known as the Satan, who, according to the New Testament, "masquerades as an angel of light" (2 Corinthians 11:14, NIV) in order to deceive and corrupt via his counter-narrative agenda (Revelation 12:9).

Cyborgs, Uploads, and Humanity+

The Biblical view of the human also challenges and affirms modern transhuman pursuits. Because humans are holistic creatures whose biology and consciousness are tied together, it is impossible for the mind to be separately uploaded to a digital realm apart from the body. Immortality, then, is only possible when we are tethered to the source of immortality, which is God.

However, trans-humanism does get something right—our current physical state is replete with limitations and flaws. Biblically, these limitations exist as a result of separation from oneness with our creator. And the solution to this separation is actually a new human fused, not with cyber-technology but with divinity. Jesus is this new human, and in him, a new species, in restored oneness with God, is being formed for a new world in which the present moral, intellectual, and physical limitations of our fallen natures are forever removed.

How Does this Help Make Sense of God's Justice and Judgment?

As mentioned above, the consciousness of all who have died is held in a state of suspension until the judgment; at which point, some are marked for eternal reanimation (the saved) and others for eternal annihilation (the lost). But what exactly does this eternal annihilation mean? Read the following texts:

| 1 Timothy 1:17 | Ezekiel 18:4 | Ecclesiastes 9:5–6, 10 |
| 1 Timothy 6:13–16 | Matthew 10:28 | Psalm 115:17. |

Okay, so those texts don't exactly answer the question. That's because we are going to dive into this final divine act of judgment in the next chapter. But here is what we can gather so far: Human consciousness is mortal, not immortal. Only God is immortal—which means that if a person dies disconnected from God, they cannot live forever because they are not plugged into the source of "forever." The only logical conclusion is that whatever the fate of the wicked is, *it's not going to be eternal conscious torment.*

And this makes sense. Because God's cosmic neighborhood has no place for injustice, those who have clung to the impulse of self are not allowed to live on. Even if God let them into heaven, it's not like they would be happy living eternally in a world where other-centered love is the cornerstone of life and society. So, God has drawn a line in the sand, a line which oppression and suffering is not allowed to cross. And those who cling to the impulse that perpetuates disharmony will not be allowed into the new earth.

However, the good news that we have seen so far—especially in the vision of Daniel 9—is that redemption is available to all of us. Regardless of how dark our past, we are all invited to a new beginning. All invited to a rebirth. The promise of salvation extends even to the worst of us.

For this is how God loved the world: He gave his one and only Son, so that everyone who believes in him will not perish but have eternal life. God sent his Son into the world not to judge the world, but to save the world through him.

John 3:16-17, (NLT)

REFLECT

Creator engineered a beautiful, interconnected ecosystem of reality to which we belong. He also created our plane of existence to intersect relationally with his own. This means the spiritual and physical dimensions are in a dance with each other. Both matter not only on their own, but in relationship to one another. This means that as human beings, we are not here by accident but on purpose. We belong to reality. We are integral parts of its emerging beauty. We are meant to occupy this plane and take up space, not only for a short time, but for eternity. This holistic view of ourselves and of the world is unique to the biblical mind and anchors our meaning and destiny forever. But it also helps us make sense of one of Christianity's most disturbing teachings: the doctrine of eternal hell. We will turn to this in the next chapter.

CONNECT

Review _____
_____

Open _____
_____

Ask _____
_____

Decide _____
_____

ENGAGE

Scan the QR code to watch this chapter's accompanying Reflection video.

SCAN ME: THE MORTALS

8. THE FIRE

As we near the end of the story of scripture, we find ourselves standing before the throne of God in Revelation 20. The wicked have surrounded the New Jerusalem for war. They want to take the city by force and claim what is not theirs. The principles of Babylon are alive and well within them. They are filled with the envy of Cain and the wickedness of the antediluvian world. United like those who built the tower of Babel, they once again gather to oppose the God of heaven. Led by the Satan himself, they organize themselves to seize the city of love.

The tension in the story is painful. The city, in one sense, is theirs. It was a gift for every human being. The qualification for entry was simple: faith in Jesus. There was nothing exceptional or impressive that they had to do to enter the city because the city was theirs, and salvation was for them. But they rejected it. And now they find themselves outside the city longing to be inside.

The contrast here is also important. The army outside the city is filled with the wicked-lost. But this does not mean that the people inside the city are the saintly knights of the human story. The wicked-lost are on the outside yes. But on the inside, we find the wicked-saved. There are murderers and thieves, liars and oppressors, drunkards and extortioners within the city. And the ones outside the city are no different. Once again, the point of distinction is that those within the city surrendered their brokenness to God. They received his grace and forgiveness, trading the black pages of their past with the spotless record of Jesus. And as a result of this exchange, they entered into a transforming, recreating relationship with God. Paul put it this way:

> *Unjust people who don't care about God will not be joining in his kingdom. Those who use and abuse each other, use and abuse sex, use and abuse the earth and everything in it, don't qualify as citizens in God's kingdom. A number of you know from experience what I'm talking about, for not so long ago you were on that list. Since then, you've been cleaned up and given a fresh start by Jesus, our Master, our Messiah, and by our God present in us, the Spirit (1 Corinthians 6:9–11, The Message).*

Because the way to eternity is available to every human being, no one needs to fear judgment. The way is free. Jesus is the portal to restored oneness with God. He is the way to eternal life. Regardless of how far you have been, you can be reconnected, recreated, and re-birthed into the new humanity of Jesus. All you have to do is say "yes" to the invitation.

But what about the wicked-lost? What is their eternal fate? There are two common views in Christian thought: one suggests that they are tormented in fire for the ceaseless ages of eternity; the other view suggests that God forever deletes their consciousness from existence. But which is true?

The answer, of course, needs to be found in the Bible. Recall from the previous chapter that there are different ways in which people have perceived reality: Atheist, Pagan, Eastern/Greek, and Transhuman. Among these perceptions, the Greek view plays a major role in how we interpret the Bible's teaching on hell.

But the Bible doesn't teach any of these views. Rather, it teaches that there is a holistic connection between the spiritual and the physical, so much so that they cannot be separated. Thus, when a person dies, the spirit (breath / spark of life) returns to God, the soul (a person's consciousness) enters a suspended state the Bible calls "sleep," and the body returns to the dust of the ground. All three elements of human life (spirit, body, consciousness) cannot function independently of one another. The three must be together at the same time for there to be a life. As a result, when a person dies, the soul does not float off to some other realm (this is the Greek view) or get placed into another body (the Eastern view / reincarnation). Instead, it goes into a temporary unconscious sleep. At the resurrection, the breath is returned to the body and the soul animates once again.

But what happens at the final destruction? In order to fully answer this question, let's explore three Biblical concepts: Destruction, Eternal Fire, and Eternal Life.

DESTRUCTION

Read the following verses: Malachi 4:1–3; Psalm 37:10; Isaiah 47:14; Matthew 25:41. What do they say about the fate of those who hold onto sin?

_____
_____
_____

Notice that, according to these writers, the wicked will not live forever in torment. Instead, they will be completely annihilated.

ETERNAL FIRE

However, doesn't the Bible say the lost will be punished with eternal fire?

How do we make sense of this contradiction? Read and discuss Jude 7, 2 Peter 2:6, Jeremiah 17:19–27, and Deuteronomy 4:24.

_____
_____
_____

In scripture, the fire is always eternal, and its effects are also eternal. But because mankind is not eternal, those who have embraced the impulse of self as their governing system are annihilated. They do not suffer for all eternity.

ETERNAL LIFE

In order for the popular doctrine of hell to be true, then both the just and the unjust must have eternal life. One in heaven and the other in hell.

Explore the following Bible promise: John 3:16. Who, according to this promise, has eternal life? And what happens to those who don't have it?

_____
_____
_____

According to the Bible, the popular view of hell as an eternal place of torment is false. Not only does it contradict the verses which clearly speak of destruction, it also contradicts the biblical cosmology where the body and soul cannot exist independently of one another.

So then, why do so many believe this? The answer takes us to a time when the practice of understanding scripture via the lens of Greek thought became the norm. This paved the way for the teaching of eternal, conscious torment to become the central view of eternal judgment in the church. Through its centuries of power, the historic church used this false teaching to control and manipulate both emperors and peasants.

Tragically, this teaching has done more to cause people to doubt the goodness and love of God than any other false teaching around. So, while the church-empire lost its power a long time ago, its influence as the proponent of lies about God continue to this day. As we have seen, Revelation predicts its resurgence toward the end of time. Even to the very end, the Satan's agenda is to tell lies about God. Those outside the city believe the lies. Those within have learned to reject them in favor of the truth God is revealing about himself through his transparent self-revelation.

But God is Still Killing People Isn't He?

As good as the realization that hell is not a place of eternal, endless torture, which God somehow engineered and props up, is, we are still left with an uncomfortable tension. God is love, and yet in the end we can't seem to get away from the fact that there is a portion of the human species that he "deletes from existence" or "annihilates." In fact, these terms can be irritating because they feel like politically correct ways of saying what we don't want to say—that God kills people, end of story. What do we do with this tension?

Investigate the ideas presented in the following verses: Exodus 24:17, Deuteronomy 4:24, and Isaiah 33:14–16. What do the say about the nature of God's presence?

_____
_____
_____

Notice that in these verses God is not depicted as using fire but as being fire. And according to Isaiah, the only kind of people who can dwell in the fire are those whose lives are in harmony with the way of love—this is the new humanity. The self-centered cannot survive the fire because it is the pure presence of divine love that absorbs and incinerates injustice and evil.

This helps give us a different angle to understanding the fire that destroys the wicked. According to these verses, the fire is God himself; which means, as one author put it, *heaven and hell are both in the same place: God's presence.* For the self-absorbed, the fire of God's presence destroys and consumes. For those who have been reborn into the way of love, the trans-humanity of Jesus, the all consuming love of God's presence becomes their eternal home.

Recall that pure love and the impulse of self cannot occupy the same spatial location in the same way that light and darkness cannot. Once the light comes on, darkness is absorbed and ceases to be. And in a sense, this is how the final judgment takes place. God steps out from behind the veil. He is no longer hiding the glory of his presence. And those who have clung to the impulse of self, to the way of the Satan, will no longer have a place in this new cosmos. Love will annihilate all selfishness and delete it from reality forever. But those who have embraced love will thrive in the new dimension, and the fire of God's presence will be, not their end but their new beginning.

So as we draw to the close of the story in Revelation 20, the lost surround the city to take it by force. The next thing John sees is God sitting on a great, white throne, and all the wicked are judged according to their works (v11). Then, fire comes down from heaven and consumes them (v9). In short, God's very presence is unveiled and it consumes and removes all sinful anomalies and deviations of design from reality. The cosmos is now cleansed of all injustice and oppression and fully restored to its original, symphonic design. A new age begins.

REFLECT

God is a just God. While it is true that heaven will not be populated by those who have clung to sin and its scaffolds of injustice, it is equally true that God will not torment anyone for eternal ages. Eternal life is a gift that God gives to those who have embraced the new humanity in Jesus. The wicked do not receive this gift. Instead, God gives them what they most desire—eternity without him, which is eternal death. Because God himself is the fire, the wicked cannot live in his presence. Rather than torment them with eternity in his presence, God gives them justice. The universe is cleansed of both sin and sinner. There will never again be a Babylon, an "other" horn or a beast. No more lies about God. No more suffering. No more injustice or oppression. The universe now sighs in relief—*It is finished*.

CONNECT

Review _____
_____

Open _____
_____

Ask _____
_____

Decide _____
_____

ENGAGE

Scan the QR code to watch this chapter's accompanying Reflection video.

SCAN ME: THE FIRE

9. THE WEDDING

With sin and sinners gone forever, our universe enters a new age. It is an age in which love is, once again, the design by which all of reality operates. And, of course, it is an age filled with joys far beyond anything we have ever experienced or could possibly imagine. Unlike the Greek conception of heaven, which is ethereal, the Bible pictures heaven as a physical recreation. This means eternity will be similar to life as we know it, only devoid of the sin that has brought suffering and injustice. We will eat, build and govern as we do now, but love will be at the center of everything we do. The best part is, this is an age that will never end.

In other words, the story is far from over. The great controversy between good and evil is just a chapter in a much larger story. It is not the story in its entirety. As a result, the final words of Revelation introduce us not to the end of the story, but to a never-ending conclusion. This eternal end is introduced with these words:

Then I saw a new heaven and a new earth; for the first heaven and the first earth passed away, and there is no longer any sea. And I saw the holy city, new Jerusalem, coming down out of heaven from God, made ready as a bride adorned for her husband. And I heard a loud voice from the throne, saying, "Behold, the tabernacle of God is among men, and He will dwell among them, and they shall be His people, and God Himself will be among them, and He will wipe away every tear from their eyes; and there will no longer be any death; there will no longer be any mourning, or crying, or pain; the first things have passed away" (Revelation 21:1–4, NASB).

After John saw this, an angel came to him and said, "Come here, I will show you the bride, the wife of the Lamb" (Revelation 21:9, NIV). And from that moment forward, John is given a tour of what heaven will be like.

Take the time to read and discuss Revelation 21:10–22:4. Summarize what John saw.

_____
_____
_____

The New Jerusalem is certainly a beautiful city. Its brilliance is like a very costly stone, as a stone of crystal-clear jasper. The city is pure gold, like clear glass. The foundation stones of the city wall are adorned with every kind of precious stone and the twelve gates are twelve pearls. The street of the city is pure gold and there is a river of life, clear as crystal. The tree of life bestrides the river which flows through its center, and every month it yields a different fruit.

But don't get lost on the surface of material beauty. In many ways, these pictures of gems and stones—while certainly real—are archetypes of something deeper. Notice that while precious stones are used as rare articles of economic strength in our day, in heaven they are used as foundations and roads. In other words, the new creation will be so abundant that the things we now consider to be rare and immensely valuable will, in the new city, make up the paths under our feet. This points us toward an age of economic abundance, in contrast to the scarcity of our wounded planet. The crystal-clear river also hints at the environmental purity we will enjoy: the tree of life at the existential and eternal significance of a universal community anchored in love and the simple, adventurous pleasures for which we were designed.

But even this is not the main point of the vision. Instead, the entire film moves us toward its epicenter—the throne of God and of the Lamb. It is in the midst of the city that John hears that God's dwelling place is now with men. This is a fitting end to a story of sin, separation, and broken sanctuary. All is restored down to the most important detail: God's desire to be with us is finally realized. We will see his face at last, and we will live (sanctuary) with him forever.

Notice also the size of the New Jerusalem. According to the angel, the city is over 2,320 kilometers long, wide, and tall. This makes the city nearly the size of Australia, or about half the size of the US.

In addition, outer space is just about 100km above the surface of the earth today. This city is so tall it literally reaches over 2,000km into space. In other words, it's a colossal city. But why?

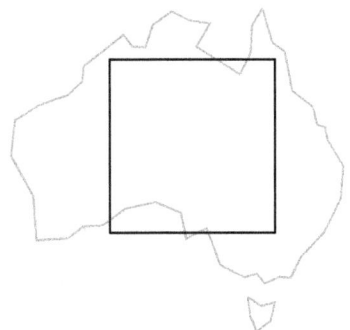 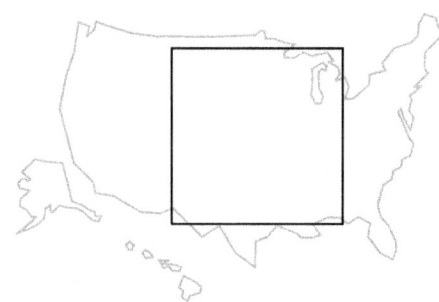

Read and discuss 1 Timothy 2:4; Hebrews 2:9; and 2 Peter 3:9, 18.

_____
_____

God wants all of humanity to be saved. From the beginning he has worked to bring us back to himself and has prepared a city for us to live in. As amazing as heaven sounds, we have to remember the promise that "No eye has seen, no ear has heard, and no mind has imagined what God has prepared for those who love him" (1 Corinthians 2:9, *NLT*). But this we do know: God's sanctuary nature will be fully revealed as we enter into an eternity in which God himself will be among us and with us.

This brings us to the end of the scriptures overarching narrative. However, there is so much we haven't yet explored. The Bible is a living, breathing, infinite book from which we can continue to derive truth and significance for ages to come. So as our present book concludes, consider using the themes we have explored as a lens through which you can go back and read the Bible for yourself. Begin with Genesis and work your way forward until you have cruised through the entire narrative.

Speaking of the entire narrative, let's recap what we have learned through our road trip. We began at the beginning by visiting with a God who is community—an eternal three and yet one who lived in an eternal experience of agape love. We saw how this love then forms the foundation for creation and our very existence. But the love was broken with the rebellion, and man was separated from God, our reason for existence. But God had a plan to restore us back to himself and heal the broken love within us. Jesus—who is God—became a man and lived as one of us. He conquered the separation by becoming the bridge that reconnects us with God. He conquered broken love by living a life of perfect love. He conquered fallen empire by living a life of unbending faithfulness to the Kingdom of God. He conquered the Satan's claim over humanity by becoming the second Adam and defeating him in every point. And he conquered death by returning to life three days after his crucifixion.

And now, because he lives and stands for us, we can enjoy the fruit of his victory. In Jesus, we are restored back to relationship with God. There is no longer a separation. In Jesus, we are restored back to perfect love; we are no longer slaves of self. In Jesus, we are royalty in the kingdom of heaven. We no longer belong to fallen empire because we have been adopted out of the family of earth and now belong to the family of heaven. In Jesus, we are no longer slaves of selfhood's prince and are free from his claim over us. Our sins are pardoned, our past erased, our future secured. We are now a new humanity. And in Jesus, we are no longer bound by death; for we belong to the one who conquered death.

This powerful message became the church's story to tell. But just like Israel of old, the church lost its way. For over 1000 years, the church was corrupted into a religio-political empire that, in many ways, became the apex of human empire. But the truth never died. All throughout the reign of the church-empire, the underground church remained a whisper, which emerged with full force in the wake of a protest launched by the infamous priest, Martin Luther. Shortly after, the church-empire collapsed, and the message of God's heart continued to spread. And now, in our modern age, the final chapter of this entire story approaches. This final chapter is God's final act to save humanity by restoring the story of his heart and spreading it through the earth.

But this final chapter is to be riddled with conflict. Revelation depicts a final struggle in which the totality of human empire will tether, to rage against the kingdom and people of God—those whose hearts are in harmony with love (keep his commandments) and whose entire identity is centered in Jesus, the new human. But it's no use. Love is too powerful, and love wins.

In the midst of this tension, Jesus returns for his people and the final judgment culminates in the complete and total eradication of human empire and the impulse of self. Love once again becomes the law of the universe and the human heart. A new age begins.

This summary is a clean and neat synopsis of the story the Bible tells. But make no mistake—the war between good and evil is far from clean or neat. This story is far more complex, far more mysterious, and far more perplexing than we could ever imagine. It's filled with intrigue, suspense, action, war, love, romance, and deception. There are questions we can't answer, obscurities we can't even begin to explore, and even the layers we do understand we only understand in part. There is a depth to the story of God which we, as mere mortals, must never assume to exhaust. We can never place God in a box and think we have him all figured out. And even when we hold truth squarely in our hands we are confronted with how little we really know. Nonetheless, the Bible is not a novel that one can simply read. It is not a fictional tale intended to help the reader escape reality. No. It is reality. It is truth. It demands a response.

The war between love and self, good and evil, light and darkness is a war we are all familiar with. There is pain, suffering, heartache and brokenness. The horrors and atrocities of this world are daily reminders that love is not the cornerstone of humanity's government. But God has not left us to ourselves. We are loved. We are valued. And through the death of his son, God has removed every barrier between him and us, and he pursues us daily with the hope that each of us will choose to be reconciled to him.

Soon, God is to finalize the judgment of this world, and, like a cancer that ravages the human body, God will remove the sin-virus that has for so long brought untold pain and suffering upon his creation. Separation will be forever absorbed in the full restoration of cosmic relational oneness.

This return to oneness means this: God will restore our cosmos to the way in which he originally created it to be—a reality filled with creatures who live and breathe according to the law of other-centered, agape love. A place worthy of being called home.

Nineteenth century author Ellen G. White summarized the conclusion of scripture's narrative best in her book, *The Great Controversy*, when she wrote:

The great controversy is ended. Sin and sinners are no more. The entire universe is clean. One pulse of harmony and gladness beats through the vast creation. From Him who created all, flow life and light and gladness, throughout the realms of illimitable space. From the minutest atom to the greatest world, all things, animate and inanimate, in their unshadowed beauty and perfect joy, declare that God is love.[1]

---

1. Ellen G. White. "The Great Controversy," p. 678

ENGAGE

Scan the QR code to watch this chapter's accompanying Reflection video.

SCAN ME: THE WEDDING

HEALING TEACHING

The concept of heaven is often misused by Christians to justify detachment from present issues that require compassion and attention. However, the biblical vision of heaven is not there to inspire passivity toward the ecological and social crimes of our age. To the contrary, they are there to show us the kinds of things that matter to God and to the new earth he envisions. If ecological harmony and social healing are important in the new earth, believers are called to live those rhythms out in the here and now. We are not to wait to get whisked off to heaven. To the contrary, we already belong to heaven—to this new humanity and civilization. And as ambassadors and representatives of that new world, we live out its rhythms in the here and now.

THE ROAD THROUGH SCRIPTURE

Note: This timeline includes the visions of both Daniel and Revelation. Read through the PDF timelines in part 2 in order to appreciate it fully.

What you see here is a summary of the road you have just traveled. We began before creation and have reached the epilogue, at the new creation. In between, we have seen God's redemptive narrative at play in the complex back and forth of cause and effect, love and betrayal, harmony and rebellion. We have seen the war between love and empire and have glimpsed the final scenes yet to come. And though the story never ends, the chapter of rebellion closes like this: *Love wins*.

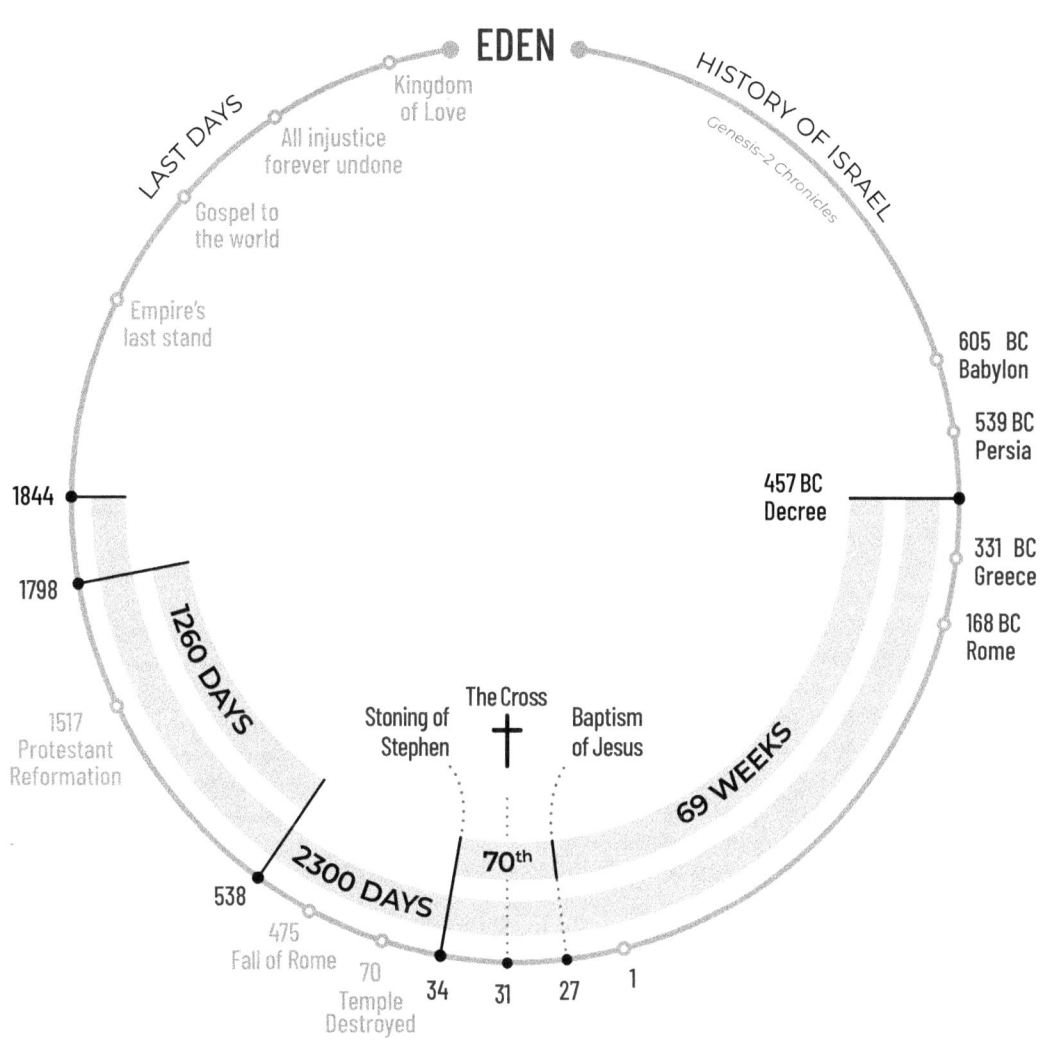

PIT STOP

Congratulations on finishing part three of *The Road*! You have officially reached the end of this series. By now, you will have learned the overarching story of the Bible from pre-creation to New Creation. This journey has taken you through the narrative of salvation, the church, and the approaching apocalypse. The battle between good and evil is soon to enter its final phases, but the conclusion has already been set. *Love wins.*

Now that this series has ended, there is another set of studies, known as "The Kingdom," that can take you from understanding the overarching story of scripture to applying it in real time. Its one thing to know the Bible's grand narrative, but it's another thing to live it out. The Kingdom is all about how to live as a member of heaven's kingdom and what that looks like in every-day life. We explore how to read the Bible for yourself, how to talk to God, how to share your faith, how to grow in your relationship with God, how to live an authentic spirituality, and more.

But before we get into that, we need to make sure that the foundation is set, so that what is to come is built on what you have already seen. So we are due for another pit stop. Again, the purpose of the pit stop is to go back to the beginning to refresh, refine, and reinforce what we have learned. Use the instructions that follow and discuss the points with your fellow travelers. By the end of this pit stop you should have a solid foundation to help you navigate the Bible on your own. Let's get started!

GOD/CREATION — WAR — RESTORATION — EMPIRE — PROTEST — NEW CREATION

SCAN ME: PART 3 PIT STOP

REFRESH

The Signs

The war of the two kingdoms continues to the end of time. But Jesus has promised that he will return and that his kingdom will bring an end to all the empires of this world. The signs of his return are everywhere, and they are hints that we are nearing that time. But one sign has yet to be fulfilled—a people filled with radical love who spread the Jesus-story everywhere they go. This group of people are so consumed by the agape of God that even in the midst of persecution they continue to tell the story. And as they do, the final events are triggered, culminating in the arrival of the Kingdom of God.

The Collapse

The Satan's war against God is not over. While we live in an age of prosperity, the Bible prophesies a catastrophe that will see a resurgence of Papal oppression and intolerance. The deadly wound is being healed, and soon the first beast, the second beast, and the dragon will unite to war against God and his church composed of those who have fallen in love with Jesus—who live, day by day, immersed in his love. As they dance with him, their hearts are molded by the Holy Spirit to love like he does. And when society collapses, Jesus depicts them as enduring in love in the midst of injustice and absurdity. This supernatural expression of agape love will continue until the gospel has reached all nations and Jesus returns to claim those who have chosen the way of love.

The Mark

As the events in Revelation 13 begin to unfold, the world will see a resurgence of religious intolerance rivaled only by the evils of the Dark Ages. The other horn will re-emerge to dominate, control, and enforce its agenda on the world. Those who disagree will be persecuted. The anti-Christ system, with its counter-narrative and alternative system of salvation, will engulf the world. The truth of God's grace and salvation will face the threat of extinction again. But in the end, love wins.

The Warnings

The three angels' messages warn us to keep our faith in Jesus and live for him alone. We are now living on the cusp of the first angel's message. Our task is to preach the good news, call people to abandon Babylon, live for Jesus only, and proclaim the reality of a present-time judgment. Soon, Babylon will fall, and the children of the *ecclesia* will be called to proclaim this to the world. Shortly after, the judgment will end, Jesus will return, and every evil empire that dwells on the earth will meet its final hour.

The Return

The first coming of Jesus may have been quiet, but his second coming will be catastrophically beautiful. When he first came, he came as a baby. When he returns, he returns as a conquering king. The corrupt and self-centered will be destroyed, but those who have loved him and waited for him will be "caught up...in the clouds to meet the Lord in the air, and so we will always be with the Lord" (1 Thessalonians 4:17).

The Millennium

God's people dwell with him in heaven, performing a work of judgment for a thousand years. When that work ends, God's city relocates to the earth, where the judgment against the wicked is executed in full. The Satan—instigator of the entire war between good and evil—is held ultimately responsible for the sin that has disrupted the harmony of God's universe for so long. He wanders the earth alone and is finally destroyed, bringing a total end to a war that has caused immeasurable suffering.

The Mortals

Creator engineered a beautiful, interconnected ecosystem of reality to which we belong. He also created our plane of existence to intersect relationally with his own. This means the spiritual and physical dimensions are in a dance with each other. Both matter not only on their own, but in relationship to one another. This means that as human beings, we are not here by accident but on purpose. We belong to reality. We are integral parts of its emerging beauty. We are meant to occupy this plane and take up space, not only for a short time, but for eternity. This holistic view of ourselves and of the world is unique to the biblical mind and anchors our meaning and destiny forever.

The Fire

God is a just God. While it is true that the unrepentant sinner will be punished for his sin, he will be punished justly. Eternal life is a gift that God gives to those who long for the kingdom of love. Those who ally themselves to the way of self do not receive this gift. Instead, God gives them what they most desire—eternity without him, which is eternal death. Because God himself is the fire, the wicked cannot live in his presence. Rather than torment them with eternity in his presence, God gives them justice. The universe is cleansed of both sin and sinner. There will never again be a Babylon, an "other" horn, or a beast. No more lies about God. No more suffering. No more injustice or oppression. *It is finished.*

The Wedding

"The great controversy is ended. Sin and sinners are no more. The entire universe is clean. One pulse of harmony and gladness beats through the vast creation. From Him who created all, flow life and light and gladness, throughout the realms of illimitable space. From the minutest atom to the greatest world, all things, animate and inanimate, in their unshadowed beauty and perfect joy, declare that God is love" (Ellen White, *The Great Controversy*).

REFINE

The Signs	*How much of what Jesus predicted can you see happening around you? What about the final sign of a people who love like he loves?*
The Collapse	*There is a saying that goes, "Crisis does not develop character, it reveals character." Do you agree? Disagree? And how does this phrase apply to the coming catastrophe depicted in Revelation?*
The Mark	*What does this "mark" really represent? And why does it matter?*
The Warnings	*What do you think about the systems and institutions of oppression coming to an end? How should this vision impact our relationship with human empire?*
The Return	*In light of the soon return of Jesus, what changes do you think you can make in your life and priorities?*
The Millennium	*What is the purpose of the millennial judgment?*
The Mortals	*How does the biblical view of death impact your view of yourself and the value of your existence?*
The Fire	*How does the truth about hell impact the way you picture God?*
The Wedding	*How does the story end? And what does it mean for your life right now?*

REINFORCE

In the overarching narrative of scripture, we have encountered 6 keys that help us unlock its full meaning. As our adventure draws to a close, there is one final key to be introduced. This key is also a consistent theme that strings the story of scripture along to its conclusion. It is central to the sanctuary, especially the judgment scene, and emphasizes the ultimate promise of the entire story. This key is called "Atonement," and through it we understand that all of God's actions in history are oriented toward to final and complete restoration of the universe. The spiritual vacuum is healed and, at last, "one pulse of harmony beats through the vast creation...God is love."

Trinity	*God is an eternal community of agape love.*
The Sanctuary	*God dwells "with" us in time and history.*
Design	*God's universe is built on other-centered parameters.*
Rebellion	*God is at war with the Satan and his selfish empire.*
Redemption	*God saves us through the gift of Jesus's sacrifice.*
Protest	*God reverses fallen empire through lives of protest.*
Atonement	*God restores the universe back to oneness with his heart.*

FURTHER STUDY

If you enjoyed our road trip and don't want the adventure to end, there is good news! You can now go further and explore deeper while driving in your car! Scan the QR code in the next page (top) to go premium on The Road's companion devotional app, *Withness*.

Also, don't forget you can explore the visions of Daniel and Revelation in way more detail by unlocking its secret codes and working out the timeline puzzles with the QR code in the next page (bottom).

Get ready to have your mind blown as you uncover the supernatural side of these visions and what they have to say about history, the future, and the spirit war we are immersed in.

SCAN ME: WITHNESS APP

SCAN ME: TIMELINES

www.ingramcontent.com/pod-product-compliance
Lightning Source LLC
Chambersburg PA
CBHW062137160426
43191CB00014B/2306